D0965813

Ronald Reagan

Ronald Reagan

℮

Michael Schaller

Published in Association with the American Council of Learned Societies

UNIVERSITY PRESS

2011

OXFORD
UNIVERSITY PRESS

Oxford University Press, Inc., publishes works that further
Oxford University's objective of excellence
in research, scholarship, and education.

Oxford   New York

Auckland   Cape Town   Dar es Salaam   Hong Kong   Karachi
Kuala Lumpur   Madrid   Melbourne   Mexico City   Nairobi
New Delhi   Shanghai   Taipei   Toronto

With offices in

Argentina   Austria   Brazil   Chile   Czech Republic   France   Greece
Guatemala   Hungary   Italy   Japan   Poland   Portugal   Singapore
South Korea   Switzerland   Thailand   Turkey   Ukraine   Vietnam

Copyright © 2011 by Oxford University Press and
the American Council of Learned Societies

Published by Oxford University Press, Inc.
198 Madison Avenue, New York, NY 10016

www.oup.com

Oxford is a registered trademark of Oxford University Press.

Library of Congress Cataloging-in-Publication Data
Schaller, Michael, 1947–
Ronald Reagan / Michael Schaller.
p.   cm.
"Published in Association with the American Council of Learned Societies."
Includes bibliographical references.
ISBN 978-0-19-975174-7
1. Reagan, Ronald.
2. Presidents—United States—Biography.   I. Title.
E877.S2558 2011   973.927092–dc22
[B]   2010015726

3 5 7 9 8 6 4

Printed in the United States of America
on acid-free paper

To Gail—my bridge over troubled waters

Contents

Contents

Preface

As a public and private figure, Ronald Reagan intrigued his contemporaries and challenges historians. When he became president in 1981, I wondered what in his background equipped him for the trials he would face leading a nation confronting so many domestic troubles and foreign threats. Aside from his rugged good looks, easy manner, and deep well of self-assurance, could he even understand, let alone remedy, problems like "stagflation," terrorism, and the malaise that pundits proclaimed afflicted the nation?

More than two decades have passed since Reagan left the White House. During those years, I have written extensively about the man and taught courses that examine his life and presidency. Even though I continue to question the wisdom of many Reagan-era policies, I have come to appreciate how his style and political skill reassured the nation and in many ways altered the country's political trajectory.

Reagan, as I will argue, failed to accomplish many of his stated goals, such as cutting spending, taxes, debt, and the size of government. Yet he initiated a process of change in these and other areas that continues to shape the relationship between ordinary Americans and the institutions that govern them. There may not have been an actual "Reagan Revolution," as his supporters claim, but since the 1980s America has experienced an ongoing Reagan "evolution," which can be seen in many aspects of governmental and judicial policy. Reagan's labeling of "big government" as a problem, his celebration of the market, his efforts to promote a more conservative social ethic, and his determined resistance to the Soviet Union and other enemies altered the direction of national life in ways that affected both the presidents who followed him and the nation at large.

During his eight years as president, and especially after, supporters praised Reagan as a transformative leader who, like Abraham Lincoln and Franklin D. Roosevelt, used his power to alter fundamentally the nation's direction. Even many Americans who disliked Reagan's policies agreed that he might well be the most influential president since Roosevelt, turning the nation away from many of the "big government" programs initiated during the New Deal.

Reagan received widespread praise for restoring national pride and an unembarrassed muscular patriotism that had lapsed after the debacles of the Vietnam War, the Watergate scandals, and the economic reversals of the 1970s.

Democratic Party leaders acknowledged Reagan's political skill but disparaged his ideas and programs. Clark Clifford, an influential power broker since 1948, called Reagan an "amiable dunce." Democratic Speaker of the House Thomas "Tip" O'Neill put it more gently. Questioning Reagan's understanding of his own administration's policies, O'Neill described him as better suited to be a ceremonial "king" than a president.

Biographer Garry Wills explained Reagan's self-assurance and determination in another way. Wills described Reagan as the real-life embodiment of the nearsighted Mr. Magoo. Like the cheerful cartoon character whose myopia prevented him from seeing anything either unpleasant or that did not conform to his mental map, Reagan simply plowed forward, oblivious to external realities.[1]

Satirist Phil Hartman, part of the *Saturday Night Live* television ensemble, captured Reagan's several sides in a 1987 skit. Hartman impersonated a silver-tongued but airheaded president sleepwalking through "photo ops" such as honoring the Girl Scout cookie captain of the year. But when the photographers leave, Reagan morphs into a hard-charging executive, telling aides exactly how to supply weapons secretly to anticommunist guerrillas, performing complex currency calculations in his head, and even taking a call apparently from Saddam Hussein in Baghdad (conducted in Arabic) that results, Reagan boasts, in a "lucrative deal with the Iraqis."

Yet these varied portrayals failed to account for the fact that throughout his career as an actor, governor, and president, most Americans felt comfortable with Reagan. They saw him not as a fool or an extremist but as something of an everyman who shared many of their hopes and fears. Critics who ridiculed his ignorance of complex policy issues misunderstood the source of his appeal, according to journalist Bill Moyers. "We didn't elect this guy because he knows how many barrels of oil are in Alaska," Moyers remarked in 1981. "We elected him because we want to feel good."

Reagan's presidency coincided with major changes in the economy, the erosion of support for liberalism and big government, and a crisis inside the Soviet Union that led to its demise. He shifted the language and content of American politics in a markedly conservative direction (such as replacing the term *citizen* with *taxpayer* and making taxes and regulation sound like dirty words). He also brought many religious, intellectual, social, and economic conservatives into the nation's political mainstream.

Historians remain divided about how successful Reagan's programs were in fostering domestic recovery or changing the trajectory of the Cold War. Did tax cuts and deregu-lation actually restore economic growth? If so, were there hidden costs? Did a president who preached frugality but incurred massive indebtedness symbolize hope or hypoc-risy? Were the benefits of covert intervention in Afghanistan worth the price of fostering a powerful anti-Western Islamist movement? Did Reagan's strident anticommunism and the surge in defense spending change Soviet behavior or merely coincide with events over which he had little control? How did Reagan affect the nation's long-term political culture?

Reagan spent thirty years in show business before entering politics. Responding to those who dismissed him as "just" an actor, Reagan told a journalist near the end of his presidency, "there have been times in this office when I've wondered how you could do the job if you hadn't been an actor." He recognized that in an age of instant visual communication, the ceremonial presi-dency had as much significance as the substance of policy making. *Time* magazine made this point when it described the ceremony on July 4, 1986 during which he unveiled a refurbished Statue of Liberty in New York harbor. Here was a 75-year-old man "hitting home runs...with trium-phant...ease that is astonishing and even mysterious." This president, in *Time's* words, was a "magician who carries a bright, ideal America like a holograph in his mind and projects its image in the air." Reagan laughed off those who labeled him the "Great Communicator," but in his last formal address as president in January 1989 insisted he had "communicated great things...the rediscovery of our values and common sense." In rallying the American people to "change a nation...instead we changed a world."

Acknowledgments

Several friends and scholars who critiqued early drafts of this manuscript helped make it a more accurate and, I hope, readable biography. Thanks especially to Leonard Dinnerstein, Chester Pach, and Robert Schulzinger.

Michael Schaller

Ronald Reagan

1

From Dixon to Tinseltown, 1911–1966

Ronald Wilson Reagan was born on February 6, 1911, in Tampico, Illinois, the second son of John Edward "Jack" Reagan, a shoe salesman, and Nelle Wilson, an adoring mother and homemaker. The future film actor, California governor, and fortieth president of the United States lived in a series of small Illinois towns and briefly in Chicago before his family settled in Dixon, Illinois, in 1920. Jack Reagan struggled with alcoholism most of his life, forcing the family to relocate frequently, often just ahead of the bill collector. Nelle Reagan, a devout member of the Protestant evangelical Disciples of Christ church, held the family together and encouraged her son, nicknamed "Dutch" (by his father, who said his haircut made him look like a Dutch figurine), to stay in school and participate in drama and sports. As a teenager and a young adult Reagan worked seven summers as a local lifeguard and was credited with saving seventy-seven swimmers from drowning. From 1928 until 1932 Reagan attended nearby Eureka College, a small, religiously affiliated institution, where he majored in economics and sociology or, as he later joked, athletics. As in high school, he was popular among his peers, was elected student body president, and enjoyed performing in campus plays.

Reagan attributed his lifelong optimism to his happy childhood, which he later described as "one of those rare Huck Finn–Tom Sawyer idylls." In fact, as told by Mark Twain, Huck's journey down the Mississippi River before the Civil War is a harrowing chronicle of slavery, racism, violence, alcoholism, child abuse, and superstition in which a precipitating event is an assault on the hero by his drunken father. As Garry Wills observed in his retelling of Reagan's life, Reagan subtly distorted his memory "toward small perfections, like the buildings of Disneyland."[2] Peggy Noonan, who became one of Reagan's most effective White House speechwriters, explained Reagan's outward amiability as a reaction to his emotionally fragile childhood. She "had the feeling he came from a sad house" and for the rest of his life "thought it was his job to cheer everyone up."[3] As biographer Sean Wilentz noted, Reagan spent much of his life turning himself into "someone else." The small-town midwestern boy became a Hollywood "city slicker." The liberal Democrat became a Republican conservative, and the right-wing citizen-celebrity became governor and president.

During the Great Depression, Jack Reagan supported his family in part by finding a job with the Works Progress Administration (WPA), the largest New Deal work-relief program. In appreciation, Ronald became a fervent supporter of Democratic president Franklin D. Roosevelt and memorized many of Roosevelt's best-known speeches. Long after he rejected liberalism, Reagan continued to admire Roosevelt as an inspirational leader. He used many of the president's techniques—such as intimate radio addresses—and incorporated many of FDR's trademark phrases to advance his own conservative agenda.

After graduating from college in 1932, Reagan had the good fortune to find work as a radio sports announcer, first with station WOC in Davenport, Iowa, and then with WHO in Des Moines. His resonant voice projected a warmth and sincerity that listeners found reassuring. On WHO, Reagan received details of Chicago Cubs games via teletype and then wove the information into a fluid narration. Sometimes, when the wire feed was interrupted, Reagan filled the air time with elaborate and colorful anecdotes. When the radio station switched to live coverage of the Cubs games broadcast from Chicago, many listeners informed the station manager that they preferred the embellished version delivered by Reagan.

In his youth, Reagan enjoyed reading self-improvement novels by writers such as Harold Bell Wright and Horatio Alger. In many of these stories, young men in dire straits rely on pluck, luck, and Christian faith to triumph over adversity and achieve middle-class respectability, if not wealth. Reagan later attributed his embrace of Christianity and his sunny outlook to the lessons he learned from reading Wright's *That Printer of Udell's* (1903), which tells of a small-town boy whose drunken father leaves his family to starve. The hero, Dick Falkner, leaves home for a big city, where he finds a job at a print shop, embraces Christianity, and, through his speaking skills, gains prominence, finally obtaining a political job in Washington, D.C.

To an uncanny degree, Reagan's life seemed to parallel what a later generation often dismissed as the stilted and sentimental plots of these moral allegories. In 1937, while in California to cover the Cubs spring training, he took a screen test for the Warner Brothers Studio and won a film contract. During the next four years he thrived as a player in dozens of so-called B films produced by the studio on a steady basis. As he later joked, the "producers didn't want them good, they wanted them Thursday." Reagan took direction well, learned lines easily, and was well liked by fellow actors and film executives. His on-screen character often responded to adversity with a wisecrack, and his off-screen personality mimicked his casting. In his later career this characteristic both charmed audiences and deflected any serious introspection, on or off camera.

Although most of his films were forgettable, in 1940 Reagan played the Notre Dame football star George Gipp in the movie *Knute Rockne, All American*. It became one of his most acclaimed roles. In the film, coach Rockne, played by Pat O'Brien, rallies the team by quoting Gipp's supposed dying words: "Win *just* one for the Gipper." As president, Reagan subtly altered the wording to "Win one for the Gipper" and used the tagline often to exhort Congress to pass his proposals. Also in 1940 Reagan married the actress Jane Wyman, with whom he had starred in two Warner Brothers pictures. The couple had a daughter, Maureen, in 1941, adopted a son, Michael, in 1945, and lost an infant daughter just after her birth in 1947.

Wyman's film career flourished during the late 1940s; Reagan's, on the other hand, began to decline. This, along with tensions over the amount of time he devoted to union activities, led Wyman to file for divorce in 1948. In later years, following his remarriage (Reagan was the first and, to date, only elected president to have been divorced), Reagan deflected discussion of the episode by insisting that he was not really divorced, since Wyman divorced *him*. While this might appear to be a difference without a distinction, Reagan often employed this type of passive language to distance himself from uncomfortable personal events that either contradicted his embrace of what he called "traditional family values" or called into question his honesty.

Soon after the United States entered World War II, the U.S. Army Air Corps called Reagan, who in 1937 had enlisted in the Army Reserves, to active duty. Ineligible for combat because of his poor eyesight, he served from 1942 to 1945 in an Army Air Corps film unit based near Hollywood that was created to encourage patriotism and support for American participation in the war. During this period Reagan became more politically active, joining the Hollywood Democratic Committee, which supported New Deal goals and close cooperation with allies, including the Soviet Union. Several of the wartime training and morale pictures he worked on depicted the global conflict as a form of entertainment. For example, in *This Is the Army* (1943), produced by Warner Brothers in cooperation with the military, Reagan played a corporal staging a variety show. As the film ends, the recruits march off to battle, singing in harmony.

This and other wartime films imprinted themselves deeply in Reagan's memory. Several times in the early 1980s, Reagan brought himself and an audience of customarily cynical journalists to tears recalling, in a quivering voice, the story of a pilot who sacrificed his life (and received a posthumous Medal of Honor) cradling a wounded comrade rather than choosing to bail out of a crippled plane. "Never mind, son," the pilot tells the young airman, terrified of dying alone, "we'll ride this one down together." Reagan seemed puzzled when journalists later questioned how he could possibly know what two dead men said to each other moments before their plane crashed in the middle of the Pacific Ocean. In fact, what he described had not happened at all; it was a montage of scenes from wartime movies.[4]

Although he served his country honorably, Reagan later seemed self-conscious about his lack of overseas or combat experience. Reflecting on this in his 1965 memoir, *Where's the Rest of Me?* (a line spoken by his character in the 1942 film *Kings Row*), Reagan explained that when peace came in 1945, he wanted the same thing as millions of other citizen-soldiers: to return home, rest, make love to his wife, "and come up refreshed to do a better job in an ideal world." This artful phrasing obscured the fact that his wartime service took place largely in Hollywood and that he was stationed in nearby Culver City.

On several occasions during his presidency, Reagan embellished his military record. For example, in both 1983 and 1985 he claimed to have firsthand experience of the Holocaust. In one account he described personally filming the liberation of Nazi death camps in Germany, while in another he claimed to have seen "secret films" of extermination camps made during the war. When journalists pointed out that he had not left U.S. soil during the war and no "secret films" existed, a White House aide explained that Reagan only meant to say he had been deeply moved by seeing films taken by American soldiers and later shown to the public.[5]

These inaccuracies were probably not intended consciously to deceive his audience. But they do suggest the depth of Reagan's belief in myths of individual heroism and his desire to be seen as part of the larger shared experience of what later became known as "the greatest generation." They also reveal his tenacity in holding on to an idea once he embraced it. Throughout his career, Reagan told stories of pilgrims, patriots, cowboys, Indians, and other icons of "rugged individualism" who seemed to have emerged from Hollywood film scripts. In public ceremonies, he often paraphrased the seventeenth-century Puritan leader John Winthrop, who described the new American settlements as "shining cit[ies] upon a hill," blessed by God. Reagan many times repeated a story about an angel who descended into Philadelphia to give divine inspiration to the squabbling Founders as they debated the text of the Constitution. Even the Strategic Defense Initiative (SDI) antimissile program he proposed in 1983 bore a striking resemblance to the plot of the 1940 film *Murder in the Air*, which featured Reagan as a special agent with the evocative name

"Brass Bancroft" assigned to protect the "inertia projector," a ray that stopped enemy aircraft.[6] In evoking these myths and symbols, he sounded sincere and persuasive, in large part because he believed what he said.

Between 1945 and 1965 Reagan made nearly two dozen additional films, but he never commanded "star" power. In the late 1940s he became active in the Screen Actors Guild (SAG), an actors' union, serving first as a board member and later as president from 1947 to 1952, and again in 1959–60. Although he campaigned for Democratic political candidates in 1948, including President Harry Truman and Minneapolis mayor Hubert Humphrey (in his Senate campaign), Reagan, like many Americans, became increasingly fearful of communist influence at home and abroad and as a result grew to distrust some members of the Democratic Party. After a bitter strike (which he opposed) by a pro-communist Hollywood union, Reagan criticized left-leaning actors, directors, and writers as potential Soviet agents sent by Josef Stalin to brainwash Americans. Sometimes he compared them to renegade Indians in western films. Both openly and as a confidential FBI informant, he helped Hollywood studios purge and blacklist accused leftists.

In 1952, three years after his divorce from Jane Wyman, Reagan married another actress, Nancy Davis. They remained devoted to each other throughout Reagan's life. Nancy's father, Dr. Loyal Davis, a prosperous and politically conservative Chicago surgeon, may have influenced the rightward drift of his new son-in-law, already in motion because of Reagan's fervent anticommunism and his displeasure at the high federal income tax bracket he fell into. This second marriage produced two children, Patricia, born in 1952, and Ronald Jr., born in 1958.

The extremely close emotional bond between the couple seemed to leave little room for their four children. Although Ron, Jr., did not, Patti, Michael, and Maureen all wrote books and told stories that described their relationship with their parents as often cold and distant. The title of Michael Reagan's published account, *On the Outside Looking In* (1988), sums up his siblings' experiences as depicted in their memoirs.[7]

Reagan's endorsement of Republican presidential nominee Dwight D. Eisenhower in 1952 signaled the end of his political allegiance to the Democratic Party. In 1954 he began an eight-year career working as an "ambassador of goodwill" for the General Electric Corporation. Reagan appeared on the weekly television drama series *GE Theater* and traveled around the country for the consumer products giant, delivering thousands of after-dinner speeches at factories and local business forums. (In 1965–66 he hosted another TV series, called *Death Valley Days*.) Year in and year out, in speeches he wrote himself, Reagan warned audiences about the perils of big government, creeping regulation, and communism. Corporate leaders, he argued, defended American freedom despite the burden of high taxes, impediments to the free market, and other antibusiness measures imposed by Democrats. In spite of the serious nature of his talks, Reagan's self-deprecating style, replete with anecdotes and humor, conveyed an upbeat rather than gloomy message. These speeches closely resembled his later presidential language.

In 1962 GE ended its relationship with Reagan. In addition to *GE Theater*'s declining ratings, the company had concerns about Reagan's increasingly vocal political stance and rumors of a Justice Department probe of his activities during his Screen Actors Guild presidency. Allegations swirled that as SAG president Reagan cut a deal with the talent agency MCA that allowed MCA to represent actors as their agents even while it produced shows in which they appeared—an apparent conflict of interest. When called before a grand jury in 1962, Reagan said he could not remember the events. No formal charges resulted, but the incident tarnished his "aw shucks" screen image.

In spite of the anticommunist crusade identified with Senator Joseph McCarthy in the early 1950s, the "mainstream" of the Republican Party followed the lead of the more moderate Dwight D. "Ike" Eisenhower after his election as president in 1952. Eisenhower accepted many New Deal tenets, such as Social Security, minimum wage laws, and farm subsidies.

The American people, Ike told his brother Milton, considered these settled policies, and any party or politician who tried to abolish them would be consigned to oblivion.

But not all members of the GOP adhered to what Ike's supporters called "modern Republicanism." William F. Buckley Jr., founder of the magazine *National Review* in 1955, used his publication as a forum to encourage conservative intellectuals to propose alternatives to what Arizona Senator Barry Goldwater ridiculed as Ike's "dime-store New Deal." Buckley and his contributors strove to bridge the gap dividing "libertarians," who believed in small government and market-oriented outcomes, and "traditionalists," who argued that government should impose a religiously based moral order on individual behavior. Buckley and his acolytes insisted that big government (defense aside) and the welfare state undermined human autonomy, morality, and economic freedom. In place of the isolationist foreign policy voiced by an earlier generation of conservatives, Buckley advocated a militant anticommunism that challenged the Soviet Union and went beyond mere "containment" of communism.

Like many residents of the so-called Sunbelt, the region that stretches from the Southeast, around the Gulf of Mexico, through the Southwest to southern California, Reagan saw dire threats coming from what he called "big government collectivism." Although major government programs like the G.I. Bill, veterans' home loans, highway construction, and heavy defense spending had sparked dynamic economic growth in the Sunbelt, conservatives remained wary. In their view, government collectivism eroded traditional values by foisting liberal curricula on public schools, undermining religious authority, imposing federal rules (like desegregation) on local institutions, and interfering with the free market through welfare programs and income redistribution schemes. Some even saw the hand of communism in a federal campaign to fluoridate drinking water. These initiatives, Sunbelt conservatives argued, fostered rising levels of crime, promiscuity, and divorce.[8]

Many Sunbelt conservatives, including those in Orange County, south of Los Angeles, also professed faith in evangelical Christianity. They envisioned an imminent battle between the forces of good and evil, followed by the return of Jesus, who would gather believers in heaven and consign nonbelievers to oblivion. Evangelical Christians faulted national leaders in both major parties for negotiating and compromising with the evils of communism and the Soviet Union rather than destroying them. In 1961 Reagan voiced this argument at a religiously focused rally in California, during which he forecast a final battle with godless communism. By 1970 he predicted (in a phrase appropriated from Lincoln) that "the world will be all slave or all free."

In the early 1960s, Reagan became a paid spokesman for the American Medical Association. On behalf of the then-staunchly conservative doctors' group, Reagan warned the public that subsidizing the cost of medical care, even for the elderly poor, would entrench socialism in the United States and undermine freedom. Unless this form of creeping "socialism" were halted, he warned, "one of these days, you and I are going to spend our sunset years telling our children, and our children's children, what it once was like in America when men were free."

Reagan formally became a Republican in 1962. Explaining his switch, he argued that he had not left the Democratic Party; rather, "the Democratic Party left me" by abandoning its support for states' rights, individualism, small government, and low taxes. In fact, outside of the South, most Democrats had rejected these tenets when they elected Roosevelt four times, Harry Truman in 1948, and John F. Kennedy in 1960. Reagan's explanation for his belated switch seemed at odds with his vigorous support for liberal Democratic candidates through 1948 and his endorsement of a moderate Republican, Eisenhower, in the 1950s.

This choice of words echoed his explanation of how his first marriage ended: He did not get divorced; rather, Jane Wyman divorced him. Often, Reagan offered explanations that distanced himself from unpleasant personal events by either pleading forgetfulness or adopting passive language. Years later, as president, he tried to minimize the seriousness of his condition when he underwent surgery in 1985 to remove a cancerous colon tumor. He told journalists that it was his colon, not he, that had cancer. When apologizing for his errors in the Iran-Contra scandal in 1987, he insisted that whatever the facts, in his "heart" he had done nothing wrong.

Sunbelt conservatism burst onto the national scene in 1964, when Arizona Senator Barry Goldwater secured the Republican presidential nomination. Despite his supporters' hopes, Goldwater proved a divisive candidate, even within the GOP. The incumbent, Lyndon Johnson, effectively portrayed him as a grouchy and dangerous extremist determined to roll back New Deal reforms like Social Security and eager to unleash a nuclear war. For Reagan, however, Goldwater's candidacy provided a national forum.

Late in the senator's faltering campaign, Reagan delivered a televised fund-raising speech titled "A Time for Choosing." By turns, Reagan's speech was humorous and indignant, as he spoke of bloated bureaucracies and the government's threat to personal freedom. Brazenly lifting phrases made famous by Franklin Roosevelt, Abraham Lincoln, and Winston Churchill, Reagan declared: "You and I have a rendezvous with destiny. We can preserve for our children this, the last best hope of man on earth, or we can sentence them to take the first step into a thousand years of darkness. If we fail, at least let our children and our children's children say of us we justified our brief moment here. We did all that could be done." He fleshed out the address with criticism of high taxes and the growing national debt, asserting that the "Founding Fathers" knew that "government does nothing as well or as economically as the private sector of the economy."

Johnson and his fellow Democrats crushed Goldwater and the Republicans nationally. Nevertheless, Goldwater made critical inroads among white Southerners, winning five states in the old Confederacy (along with his native Arizona) and cracking the Democrats' long domination of the South. It was Reagan, however, who was heralded as the informal "winner" among Republicans and celebrated as the emerging face of the conservative movement. Where Goldwater grimaced and scowled, Reagan smiled and cajoled. Although his core ideas resembled those held by Goldwater, Reagan communicated them with an inspirational ease developed over years of speaking on what he jovially called the "rubber chicken circuit." Within a few months of Johnson's triumph, a group of wealthy California businessmen, including car dealer Holmes Tuttle, drugstore executive Justin Dart, nursing home magnate Charles Z. Wick, and oil and electronics entrepreneur Henry Salvatori, organized a Friends of Ronald Reagan committee to promote his candidacy for governor of California in 1966.[9]

2

Governor of California and Presidential Candidate, 1967–1980

℃

In the months before the 1966 election in California, most journalists and Democratic Party politicians disparaged Ronald Reagan as both an amateur and an extremist. Neither label fit. Reagan had sound political instincts and a keen sense of his own strengths and weaknesses. He recognized the need to define himself to the electorate by stressing a few easy-to-grasp concepts. He pledged to reduce the size and scope of government and to throw the rascals out. "I am not a politician.... I am an ordinary citizen" opposed to high taxes, government regulations, big spending, waste, and fraud, he declared in 1966. He depicted opponents as out-of-touch elitists who favored high taxes and tolerated waste and fraud. During this campaign—and for eight years as governor and eight more as president—Reagan stayed on message. He used dramatic if sometimes fanciful anecdotes to point out the excesses or absurdities of some government regulations. When speaking of liberalism, his voice oozed with contempt. If the topic was communism, he sounded resilient. Describing the plight of hard-pressed taxpayers or small business owners, he radiated empathy and recalled his own humble origins.

Recognizing that any skilled performer requires a good director as well as a credible script, Reagan worked closely with campaign consultants who understood his ability to achieve "mastery of the electronic media." As much as possible, Reagan campaigned on television, where his ability, honed over many years of acting, to deliver a well-rehearsed script in an off-the-cuff manner served him excellently. He scored an upset primary victory over former San Francisco mayor George Christopher and then faced off against two-term Democratic incumbent Edmund G. "Pat" Brown in the general election.

Brown was an accomplished governor who held centrist views. To cope with California's surging population and the growing demand for public services, he had pushed such items as the expansion of higher education, more aid to public schools, and massive freeway construction. This investment in infrastructure promoted

California's economic success and made it an attractive place to live. But to pay for these amenities, Brown and the legislature had raised state taxes. The public services were popular; the taxes were resented. Many middle-class Californians also felt uneasy about rapid social changes. Events such as the Los Angeles Watts uprising of 1965 and racial conflicts elsewhere in the state, the raucous free speech movement at the University of California's Berkeley campus, rising crime rates, and growing agitation against the Vietnam War troubled them. Even though Brown supported the war in Vietnam and condemned violent protests, Reagan hung all these resentments on his Democratic opponent.

Reagan spoke to voters mostly in broad symbolic terms, addressing issues like freedom, personal autonomy, and traditional values. He linked Brown to urban riots, welfare cheats, criminals and the judges who "coddled" them, the "mess at Berkeley," and the spoiled "bums" who protested the Vietnam War and indulged in "sexual orgies so vile I cannot describe them to you." "Hippies," he quipped, "had hair like Tarzan, look like Jane, and smell like Cheetah." But by relying as much on inspiration as denigration, Reagan easily charmed audiences. "We can start a prairie fire that will sweep the nation and prove we are number one in more than crime and taxes," he declared. This was a "dream, as big and golden as California itself."[10]

His tone of sincerity and his willingness to tell jokes on himself (when asked what kind of governor he might be, he responded "I don't know, I've never played a governor") undercut efforts by Brown and others to portray him as either a fool or a dangerous extremist. Most voters viewed Reagan as a pleasant man aroused by a range of grievances they shared. In November 1966 they swept him into office by a margin of nearly a million votes.[11]

Reagan took his oath as California's thirty-third governor on January 2, 1967, at a midnight inauguration. The odd timing, deemed auspicious by Nancy Reagan's astrologer, blocked an effort by the outgoing Brown to make some last-minute appointments.[12] Reagan's outlook was exemplified by his more widely covered inaugural speech delivered after his reelection four years later. "For many years now," he told Californians, "you and I have been hushed like children and told there are no simple answers to the complex problems which are beyond our comprehension." In truth, he countered, "there are simple answers—there just are not easy ones."[13] Initially, at least, Reagan seemed unsure of what those simple solutions actually were. Shortly after taking office, he could not answer a question from a journalist who asked about his priorities. Turning to an aide, the new governor remarked, "I could take some coaching from the sidelines, if anyone can recall my legislative program." For a while, he limited himself to ordering an across-the-board budget cut and hiring freeze for state agencies and asking state employees to work without pay on holidays. Most refused.

After an awkward start, Reagan settled into a comfortable governing style that blended conservative rhetoric with more flexible policies. He denounced student antiwar protesters and in 1969 sent the National Guard to quell disturbances at Berkeley. But despite frequent threats, he abandoned plans to slash education spending or to probe "Communism and blatant sexual misbehavior" in the state university system. Reagan blamed Brown for an inherited budget deficit and then approved the largest tax increase in state history. He praised budget cutting and reduced funding for a few programs, but during his two terms as governor, in response to population growth and continued demands for services, state spending doubled from $5 billion to $10 billion annually.

As a candidate and as governor, Reagan criticized a casual attitude toward sex and abortion, which he believed defied morality and undercut individual responsibility. Yet in 1967, when the legislature passed a law that lifted most restrictions on abortion, Reagan signed it. (He also approved a path-breaking no-fault divorce law that dropped most impediments to ending marriage.) Reagan had serious personal misgivings about the abortion reform bill and consulted with many people on either side of the issue before granting his approval. Several years later, when opposition to abortion became a litmus test among conservatives, Reagan claimed disingenuously that he had never read the law's provisions. He also blamed women and their doctors for using loopholes to carry out more procedures than he or the law anticipated.

Reagan's bold rhetoric and more cautious governance were sometimes referred to by scholars as "populist conservatism." He inveighed against "liberal elitists," whose social agenda might be well intentioned but whose policies hurt working people, encouraged dependence, and stifled initiative. But after publicly lambasting liberals, Reagan often conducted private negotiations with Democratic state legislators that yielded workable compromises. He later adapted this technique to ensure legislative success in dealing with Congress. Democratic critics found it hard to counter Reagan's rhetorical flourish, which energized conservatives both in California and nationally.[14]

Reagan and his supporters probably smiled when LSD advocate Timothy Leary declared his intention to run for governor in 1970. (Leary's arrest on drug charges ended his candidacy, but not before he persuaded John Lennon to compose a campaign song, later released as "Come Together.") Reagan easily won reelection in 1970 against Democrat Jesse Unruh, minority leader of the California State Assembly. During his second term, he promoted modest efforts designed to help the "tax payer" and punish the "tax taker." He denounced "welfare cheats" but then struck a deal with the Democrat-controlled legislature that modestly tightened eligibility standards while substantially increasing benefits for those who qualified.

Preferring to leave office on a high note, Reagan declined to run for a third term. After leaving the governorship in January 1975, he devoted much of his time to writing opinion columns and giving radio commentaries that brought him and his ideas to millions of Americans. Reagan criticized public programs as inferior to private business and insisted that independent ranchers and private entrepreneurs had carved a prosperous civilization out of the American wilderness. His description of heroic men and women taming the West obscured the fact that California, like the entire region, had thrived on massive federal construction projects that for a century had brought public water, power, roads, and defense contracts to the West.

In the years since his death, the draft texts of many of these commentaries have become available. Refuting those who claimed he relied on ghostwriters, the drafts show that Reagan wrote his own scripts and infused them with both a pungent style and a cogent political argument. Nevertheless, it would be wrong to describe these short radio scripts and op-ed essays as something like the modern equivalent of the *Federalist Papers*. Most were homilies that resembled the human-interest features often found in publications like *Reader's Digest* or the radio essays of fellow conservative Paul Harvey. Many harkened back to the moral lessons of his favorite childhood novels. They show that Reagan knew his own mind and made a strong case for his beliefs.[15]

Reagan's two terms as governor overlapped with the presidency of Richard Nixon. Although both claimed to be genuine conservatives, the two men had little respect or affection for each other. Nixon appealed to voters' resentments, especially those relating to racial issues such as school busing. His so-called southern strategy attracted southern white Democrats, northern Catholics and ethnic blue-collar voters disenchanted with the direction of racial and social changes to the GOP fold. Yet Nixon was not a "small government" advocate or foreign policy conservative. He supported the creation of several new regulatory agencies, such as the Consumer Products Safety Commission, the Occupational Safety and Health Administration, and the Environmental Protection Agency. Nixon worked with Congress to enact clean air and water laws and minority hiring set-aside programs in federal contracts. Abroad, he promoted détente (a reduction in tensions based on arms control and trade cooperation) with the Soviet Union and a historic diplomatic opening to long-isolated China. Nearly all of these initiatives angered conservatives who considered them both bad policy and moral lapses.

Although Nixon began his political career as a vocal anticommunist, he dismissed as simple-minded Reagan's talk of returning to free market economics and confronting the Soviet Union militarily. Most people who encountered Reagan found him charming, but Nixon—whom no one considered charming—described him as "strange" and "not pleasant to be around." Nevertheless, he dispatched Reagan to Taiwan in October 1971 to explain to its anticommunist leaders that the opening of China was not a betrayal of past support but an effort to enlist Communist China against the more dangerous Soviet Union. Reagan accepted Nixon's logic, but just barely.

Nixon also shocked conservatives in 1971 when he imposed wage and price controls on the economy and abandoned the dollar's link to gold. In defending these actions, he described himself as a convert to Keynesian economics, the liberal approach to active government management of the economy through borrowing, spending, and tax policies. One startled conservative economist compared Nixon's endorsement of Keynes to a thirteenth-century crusader saying "all things considered, I think Mohammed was right." Early in 1973, Nixon further alienated the right wing of his party when he reached a compromise settlement with North Vietnam that provided for an American exit from the unpopular war. Reagan, who had earlier proposed "turning [Vietnam] into a parking lot," saw this as an implicit American defeat.

Given their disgust with many of Nixon's domestic and foreign initiatives, Reagan and other conservative Republicans may have taken private satisfaction at the president's disgrace as the Watergate scandal deepened. Publicly, however, Reagan offered Nixon support until shortly before his forced resignation in August 1974. This left an unelected president, Gerald Ford, in office and created a power vacuum in the GOP that Reagan and his fellow conservatives were eager to fill.

President Ford, a moderate conservative from Michigan, disappointed the Republican right with both his selection of the liberal Republican Nelson Rockefeller to be his vice president and his continuing reliance on Nixon's chief foreign policy adviser, Henry Kissinger. Ford continued efforts to reach arms control agreements with the Soviet Union. Even though Ford vetoed many bills passed by the Democratic majority in Congress, Reagan accused him of cooperating too closely with the liberal establishment.

Reagan challenged Ford for the GOP nomination in 1976. The Californian promised that as president he would lower taxes, deregulate business, limit abortion, restore school prayer, and confront the Soviet Union more aggressively. In colorful language, Reagan condemned Ford for negotiating with Panama to return control of the canal that bisected the isthmus. "We bought it, we paid for it, and we're going to keep it," he declared.[16]

Reagan won eleven primaries, compared to Ford's seventeen, in 1976, and came within sixty delegate votes of snatching the GOP nomination away from the incumbent. His strong challenge and the close vote on the convention floor badly rattled Ford, who dropped Rockefeller from the ticket and agreed to run on a party platform that endorsed many of Reagan's positions. Despite his effort to appease conservatives, Ford lost the election to a little-known former Georgia governor, Jimmy Carter.

Carter benefited from the public's disgust with Watergate. He received cheers from audiences during the 1976 campaign when he stated that he was not a politician and would never lie to them. He also tried to win the votes of Christian Evangelicals, who had been politically apathetic. While many Democratic politicians disparaged Carter's effort, Reagan recognized the value of tapping this overlooked voter pool. By 1980 nearly everyone deemed Carter's presidency a well-intentioned failure. During the late 1970s United States–Soviet relations deteriorated, inflation spiked, the economy slowed, unemployment increased, and gasoline became both scarce and pricey. Neither Carter, a moderate Democrat, nor congressional liberals explained these problems to the public or offered a solution to them.

Inflation became a major problem as early as 1971, when Nixon imposed wage and price controls. By 1978, inflation had hit 9 percent, and it soon rose to 12 percent. Rising prices slowed business and increased unemployment, a condition dubbed "stagflation." Carter's approval rating moved in inverse direction to the rates of inflation and unemployment. By 1979 only 29 percent of voters told pollsters they approved of Carter's performance, a percentage nearly as low as where Nixon's stood when he resigned in August 1974. A year later it declined to 21 percent.

California voters had already registered their frustration with high taxes, big, unresponsive government, and insensitive politicians by voting in favor of Proposition 13 in June 1978. This initiative, promoted by anti-tax gadfly Howard Jarvis, not only rolled back property taxes, but required a nearly impossible supermajority of voters or legislators to increase future taxes. Although Reagan had not initiated the anti-tax drive or reduced taxes while governor, he embraced this grassroots movement. The vote for Prop 13, he opined, was "a little bit like dumping those cases of tea off the boat in Boston Harbor" before the

American Revolution. Reagan understood the dual appeal of the tax-cutting approach. Hard-pressed voters whose incomes had stagnated liked lower taxes, while fellow conservatives saw lower taxes translating into less money to spend on government social programs. Carter's pollster, Patrick Caddell, recognized this fact. Passage of Prop 13, he explained, "isn't just a tax revolt" but a "revolution against government."

Disillusionment turned to disgust after November 1979, when Iranian radicals occupied the U.S. Embassy in Tehran. They ultimately seized fifty-two American diplomats and embassy guards. The hostage-takers demanded the return of the exiled Shah—who had fled in January of that year following months of strikes and protests—and his money in Western banks and a U.S. apology for past meddling in Iran. Carter denounced the hostage seizure as an illegal outrage but lost public trust in the spring of 1980 as the crisis dragged on. A botched effort to rescue the Americans in April made Carter seem especially weak. Meanwhile, domestic economic problems and foreign threats energized the candidacy of Ronald Reagan.

Reagan recognized that his path to the White House required unifying the often-bickering strands of the conservative movement. As he put it in a 1977 speech, "The time has come to see if it is possible to present a program of action based on political principle that can attract those interested in the so-called 'social issues' [which he identified as "law and order, abortion, busing, (and) quota systems"] and those interested in economic issues [such as] inflation, deficit spending and big government." He hoped to combine the "two major segments of contemporary American conservatism into one politically effective whole." Reagan himself never reconciled these tensions. But he projected a sunny vision of an idyllic America impeded only by federal bureaucrats and government red tape.

Reagan skillfully turned back against the incumbent a phrase first used by Carter against Ford: the "Misery Index." This vivid term referred to the sum of unemployment and inflation, a figure that had risen steadily since 1977. Rather than stress his conservative credentials, Reagan simply asked voters if they were better or worse off in 1980 than they had been four years earlier. In a further gesture to deflect charges that he had radical ideas, Reagan tapped the moderate George H. W. Bush, his principal rival in the 1980 primaries, as his running mate once he secured the GOP nomination. His campaign focused on a promise to restore national strength and pride. "This is the greatest country in the world," he declared. "We have the talent, we have the drive, we have the imagination. Now all we need is the leadership."[17]

He assured anxious motorists lined up for fuel at service stations that the country did not have too little oil, just too many bureaucrats and regulations. Promising to bring the public "a little good news," Reagan ridiculed those who suggested "that the United States had had its day in the sun."

Many factors beyond Reagan's rhetoric or promised policies enhanced his appeal. His campaign both encouraged and benefited from a rising clamor against taxes as well as the mobilization of religious conservatives. Before 1976 most so-called born-again Christians, who lived disproportionately in the South, either did not vote or tended to vote Democratic. Carter, a deeply religious born-again Baptist, brought many of these Americans into the electoral process. By 1980 many of these born-again Christians had become disillusioned with Carter and switched their party allegiance. They were especially attracted by Reagan's opposition to abortion and gay rights and his support for school prayer, teaching "creationism" as an alternative to evolution and giving tax breaks to all-white "Christian academies."

Reagan won the election in 1980 in a three-person contest that pitted him against Carter and John Anderson, a liberal Republican congressman from Illinois who ran as an independent. Opinion polls remained close well into October. Reagan only pulled ahead of Carter after he debated the incumbent shortly before the election and came across as affable and unthreatening. Carter's failure to win the release of the Iran hostages probably doomed his candidacy.

In spite of Carter's personal unpopularity and the nation's many foreign and domestic problems, Reagan received just over 50 percent of the popular vote to Carter's 41 percent and Anderson's 7 percent. However, in the electoral vote count, Reagan trounced Carter 489 to 49. Reagan's coattails helped Republicans pick up a net gain of twelve seats in the Senate, giving them a margin of fifty-three to forty-six and control of that body for the first time since 1954. Republicans also gained thirty-four House seats. Although Democrats retained nominal control of the House, enough conservative Democrats voted with the opposition to give Republicans a working majority on most issues.

Reagan's victory was at least as much a personal achievement as an ideological one. He capitalized on an antigovernment mood that had built since the Vietnam War, the Watergate scandal, the stagflation of the late 1970s, and the humiliation of the Iran hostage crisis. When polled about their choices, only 11 percent of voters said they selected Reagan because he was a "real conservative." Most believed it was "time for a change" and went for the Republican challenger because they favored "anybody but Carter." Choosing Reagan represented a rejection of a failed incumbent and the disaffiliation of southern white and northern ethnic voters from the Democratic Party. It was not, at least not yet, the embodiment of a new conservative consensus.

3

The Reagan Presidency, 1981–1989

℃

In his inaugural address on January 20, 1981, President Reagan scoffed at those who described the United States as suffering from a national "malaise" or living in an era of limits. It was time, he declared, "for us to realize that we are too great a nation to limit ourselves to small dreams." Reagan spoke of past heroes and stressed a few easily understood economic grievances, such as inflation and a burdensome tax system. In Roosevelt-like cadences, he described an America gripped by economic terror. But salvation, he insisted, could be achieved by rejecting the tenets of policy that stretched back to the New Deal. "In this present crisis," he declared, "government is not the solution to our problem, government *is* the problem."

Moments after he took the presidential oath, Reagan announced that the Americans long held hostage in Iran had been released. Even though Jimmy Carter had negotiated the deal that finally freed them, the timing of their release seemed clear proof that America's enemies had backed down before the new president. Change already seemed to be in motion.

Reagan insisted in a diary entry that he had no intention of repealing the New Deal. Instead, he wanted to roll back the reforms enacted during President Lyndon B. Johnson's "Great Society" program in the 1960s. Medicare, Medicaid, and the Voting Rights Act, Reagan insisted, led to a bloated and overreaching federal government. One of his first acts as president was to remove a portrait of his old hero, President Harry Truman, from the Cabinet Room and replace it with a portrait of the nearly forgotten 1920s president Calvin Coolidge. An ardent believer in the unregulated market and what was even then called "traditional values" (as opposed to the looser morals of the so-called Roaring Twenties), Coolidge was often remembered for his aphorism "The business of America is business." Reagan heartily agreed.

Over the next eight years, through recession and economic recovery, intensified Cold War and a renewed dialog with the Soviet Union, Reagan forged a powerful bond with the public. Even when most Americans opposed specific administration programs, such as efforts to ban abortion, cut school aid, or fund anticommunist guerrillas in Central America, they continued to voice confidence in the president. His connection to voters transcended specific policies and tapped into a popular will to restore a sense of community, real or imagined, that had been lost since the 1960s. Even when the recession of 1981–82 and the Iran-Contra scandal of 1986–87 drove down his approval ratings, Reagan showed a remarkable ability to rebound and recapture the public's good will.

Democratic politicians and many journalists expressed wonder that presidential gaffes and fanciful anecdotes, such as blaming trees for air pollution and claiming that mothers on welfare must be faking their poverty since some allegedly drove Cadillacs and collected hundreds of thousands of dollars, had so little negative impact. Reagan's ability to shake off setbacks led Colorado Democratic representative Pat Schroeder to dub him the "Teflon President." Reagan's supporters attributed his popularity to his success in restoring national pride and prosperity and to his skill as a "Great Communicator." In their determination to praise or criticize Reagan, liberals and conservatives often ignored tactical flexibility. To achieve 75 percent of what he wanted in a pending bill, the president explained, he would happily give up 25 percent.

Just ten weeks after taking office, on March 30, 1981, a crazed gunman named John Hinckley Jr., nearly killed the president and wounded several bystanders, including press aide James Brady, outside a Washington, D.C., hotel. In the hospital emergency room, Reagan grasped his wife's hand and reprised a line attributed to boxer Jack Dempsey after he was knocked out: "Honey, I forgot to duck." In fact, Reagan's wounds were far more serious than he himself realized or the public learned at the time—he nearly bled to death. As he went into surgery, he quipped to the medical staff, "I hope you are all Republicans." This spunk was appreciated by ordinary Americans, who for so long had seen presidents as wooden men in suits with little connection to real people. After surviving the attempt on his life, Reagan told friends he believed God had spared him for a purpose. Reagan's combination of good humor and grit boosted his standing with the public and seemed an apt realization of the code name given him by his Secret Service detail: Rawhide.

During Reagan's first administration, Chief of Staff James Baker III, Baker's deputy Michael Deaver, and Counselor Edwin Meese carefully monitored the president's legislative agenda and his public appearances. (Vice President George H. W. Bush played no significant policy role. Outside of a weekly luncheon with Reagan, he and Barbara Bush seldom socialized with the Reagans.)

The triumvirate selected a so-called "Line of the Day," a coordinated message that officials used in their communication with the media and hence the public. As Deaver characterized their handling of the press, "we fed them and they ate it every day."[18]

They would set the tone for all that followed. Nearly all of Reagan's notable domestic achievements transpired during his first term, when his able staff maximized his clout with Congress and the public. No president before Reagan used television so effectively to communicate ideas and mobilize voters. As even political rivals such as Democratic House Speaker Thomas "Tip" O'Neill acknowledged, he was also highly persuasive in one-on-one encounters with members of Congress. Yet off screen or off script—without his staff's guidance—Reagan often lacked focus, clarity, and direction. Unscripted news conferences were painful to watch and were kept to a minimum.

Baker and Meese left the White House for other administration jobs after Reagan's reelection in 1984, and Deaver went into private business. Without their skilled handling, Reagan often stumbled. Several of his most controversial actions, such as trading arms for hostages in Iran in 1985–86 and visiting a cemetery in Germany in 1985 that contained the remains of Nazi SS troops, took place when his second-term team, led by Chief of Staff Don Regan, gave him faulty advice or failed to divert him from making his own poor choices.

Even his closest aides found Reagan exceptionally detached from details and often had to guess at what he wanted them to do. At Cabinet meetings Reagan frequently read from letters and inspirational stories sent him by admirers. But after a few minutes as General Colin Powell recalled, he displayed a "glassy-eyed look," compelling aides to continue without his input. Reagan's friend and economic adviser Martin Anderson recalled that the president's aides "compensated for the fact that he made decisions like an ancient king or a Turkish pasha, passively letting his subjects serve him."[19] Reagan told his spokesperson Larry Speakes that he was happiest when "each morning I get a piece of paper that tells me what I do all day long." As he put it, being president was "something like shooting a script," in which characters appeared and departed and the plot advanced.[20]

Reagan limited his personal involvement in policy deliberations to a handful of issues, such as cutting taxes, promoting his Strategic Defense Initiative missile shield, aiding anticommunist guerrillas in Central America, and speaking out against abortion. As speechwriter Peggy

Noonan observed, "Taxes and SDI and abortion were issues that captured his imagination. He could see how taxes hurt,...he could see how SDI, with a perfectly directed laser beam, could shoot down a missile,...he could see the fetus kicking away from a needle." Once he convinced himself that the Contra guerillas in Nicaragua were the "moral equivalent of the Founding Fathers" he could not imagine abandoning them.

In spite of his relaxed governing style, the public usually perceived Reagan as a decisive administrator. For example, in August 1981, seven months into his presidency and soon after his recovery from gunshot wounds, nearly 12,000 unionized air traffic controllers ignored a no-strike clause in their contract and walked off the job. The Professional Air Traffic Controllers Organization (PATCO) had endorsed Reagan's candidacy. This fact, as well as their legitimate complaints over staffing issues, made union leaders assume that the president would tolerate, if not endorse, their strike. They guessed wrong. Reagan had long since abandoned his sympathy toward organized labor and relished the opportunity to flex his muscles against a group that both he and the public saw as overpaid, arrogant whiners who had violated their signed contract. When the strikers defied his back-to-work order, the president again cited Calvin Coolidge, who, while governor of Massachusetts, condemned striking Boston policemen by declaring "there is no right to strike against public safety." The president discharged the defiant controllers and sent military personnel into airport towers to keep commercial flights aloft. Reagan's tough stance impressed the public, intimidated the labor movement, and convinced business interests that he was firmly on their side.

Reagan encouraged his Cabinet members and other agency heads to draw appointed personnel from several conservative "think tanks" that promoted alternative ideas about economic, social, and foreign policy. In place of organizations such as the Brookings Institution and the Carnegie Endowment for International Peace, which had supplied generally liberal ideas to Democratic politicians for a generation, the Reagan administration recruited bureaucrats and sought advice from the ranks of more conservative groups, such as the American Enterprise Institute, the Heritage Foundation, the Cato Institute, and the Hoover Institution.

Reagan and his administration attempted to roll back the network of social welfare programs enacted since the New Deal; limit the role of federal courts in promoting civil rights and liberties; reduce regulation of business, banking, and the environment; cut federal income tax rates; and encourage a conservative social ethic regarding reproductive rights, drug use, and the role of religion in public life. Reagan emphasized removing what he saw as the dead hand of government regulation from the private sector, believing this would unleash market forces, create new wealth, and foster greater equality. Finally, by "rearming America" he would challenge Soviet advances in the Third World and ultimately defeat what he called "the evil empire."

As a candidate and upon taking office, Reagan criticized the nearly $1 trillion national debt as "mortgaging our future and our children's future." The nation must stop living beyond its means, he explained, and concentrate on the essentials. He pledged to cut the "bloated" federal bureaucracy and reduce the tax burden that stifled individual and business initiative. Reagan rejected the Keynesian economic theory dominant in America since the 1930s. Instead of Keynes' idea of promoting growth in periods of recession by having the government boost demand in the private sector through deficit spending, Reagan embraced a controversial theory known as "supply-side economics." This notion held that the best way to generate increased economic activity was to reduce taxes and regulation on business and reduce income taxes on high earners. Allowing businesses and the wealthy to keep more of their own money would, he maintained, generate increased economic growth and easily make up for lower tax rates. Some supply-side advocates doubted that

Reagan understood the theory behind their claim. But they knew he would find it appealing, because for decades, he had criticized high tax rates as a disincentive to work.

The president unveiled his economic package of tax and spending cuts to Congress in February 1981. It contained substantial reductions on income and business tax rates; lowered capital gains, estate, and gift taxes; shifted some social service expenditures to the states; and cut back on parts of the federal bureaucracy that regulated business, the environment, and public health. Although critics sometimes accused Reagan of being lazy, he pressed hard for passage of his economic and related defense programs. During his first four months in office he met with members of Congress seventy times to lobby for his budget proposals. He appealed to the public to bring pressure on their representatives and enlisted the support of about three dozen conservative southern Democrats, the so-called Boll Weevils, who held the balance of power in the nominally Democratic House of Representatives. In return for their votes, Reagan offered not to back their Republican challengers in the next election.

The Omnibus Budget Reconciliation Act of 1981 passed the House and Senate on July 31. It cut expenditures for fiscal year 1982 by nearly $35 billion and over 1982–84 by about $140 billion. Defense spending received a big boost, while social programs for lower-income Americans were hit hard. Although middle-class entitlements like Social Security and Medicare survived more or less intact, Food Stamps, school lunch programs, public housing subsidies, and job training took major hits.

Two weeks later Reagan signed into law the Economic Recovery Tax Act, which contained the largest tax cut in U.S. history. Over five years the revenue loss to the Treasury totaled $750 billion. The bill reduced personal income tax rates by 25 percent in three annual increments, cut capital gains and estate taxes, and reduced business taxes. Several industries, such as oil, received numerous benefits.

"Reaganomics," as headline writers dubbed the president's approach, is celebrated by conservatives for restoring economic growth and broadening prosperity. In his 1981 inaugural speech, Reagan condemned big spenders for "mortgaging our future and our children's future." The nation must stop "living beyond its means" or it would eventually face disaster. Nevertheless, Democrats and other liberal critics question whether the president's policies had much to do with recovery and insisted that the nation paid a high price for modest results. Essentially all both sides agree on is that the country experienced a steep recession in 1981 and 1982, followed by a decade of economic expansion.

Among the most important economic events of the 1980s was the taming of the country's inflation, which had reached 12 percent by the time Reagan took office. Credit for this lay mostly with Federal Reserve Chairman Paul Volcker, who, near the end of the Carter administration, imposed high interest rates on loans that eventually pushed back inflation to 4.4 percent. A steep decline in world oil prices during the 1980s also spurred recovery. Although it was natural for the president to take credit for these successes, Reaganomics had little to do with either.

Reagan is fondly remembered for his advocacy of lower taxes, smaller government, and reduced spending and debt. Although he spoke forcefully in favor of these policies (if the trillion-dollar debt he inherited in 1981 were a pile of silver dollars, he asserted, it would stretch halfway to the moon!), he seldom followed his own advice and never sent a balanced budget proposal to Congress. During the 1980s federal income tax rates declined, most significantly for the wealthiest 20 percent of taxpayers. For most other Americans, increased payroll, Social Security, and state taxes meant that they paid nearly the same total tax bill in 1989 as in 1981. Federal income taxes, as a share of national income, held steady at about 19.4 percent throughout the decade.

Economic growth from 1982 to 1989 included the creation of about 16 million new jobs and a doubling in size of the Gross Domestic Product (GDP). These achievements, however, were impressive mostly when compared to the dismal years of 1978–82. The economy actually produced more jobs and grew faster during the 1960s, most of the 1970s, and in the 1990s than it did in the Reagan years.

As a candidate Reagan had condemned the annual budget deficits and the swelling national debt accumulated by his predecessors during the 1970s. But their overspending paled in comparison to his. Because lower tax rates did not yield significantly more revenue, as supply-siders had predicted, and because of rising military spending, the annual federal budget deficit grew to record levels of over $200 billion under Reagan, as compared to a shortfall of $80 billion in Carter's final year. By 1989 the cumulative national debt had tripled to nearly $3 trillion. The fanciful pile of silver dollars would now reach the moon and come half-way back.

Nor did Reagan shrink federal spending or the number of government employees. More civilians worked for the federal government in 1989 than in 1981. Federal spending as a share of GDP remained virtually unchanged (at about 22 percent) throughout the 1980s. A few presidential advisers grew so concerned about the flow of red ink that in 1982 and 1983 they prevailed on Reagan to quietly approve major tax increases, which he preferred to call "revenue enhancements." This, along with increased

Social Security levies, negated much of the celebrated tax cuts of 1981, at least for most taxpayers.[21]

The president generally avoided discussing the specifics of his budget or the nation's economy. He guessed, correctly, that the public liked the idea of tax cuts now but lost little sleep thinking about how future deficits would be paid for. Even when the United States went from being the world's largest creditor nation to the largest debtor— paying for tax cuts and weapons purchases with money borrowed from Japan and Germany—and as its foreign trade imbalance grew worse, Reagan maintained a sunny disposition. When asked by a journalist to explain the deterioration of the U.S. trade balance, he simply denied that it was so. When asked midway through his presidency about past promises to cut spending and balance the budget, he described it as a "goal," not a promise. Significantly, when he endorsed a proposed constitutional amendment to mandate a balanced budget, he insisted that it apply only to future presidents.

Businesses benefited from both tax and regulatory reductions during the Reagan years. For example, the Justice Department adopted a more relaxed attitude toward monopoly, dropping antitrust suits against corporate giants like IBM and permitting the merger of many former competitors. The Interior Department, led by James Watt, lifted many restrictions on oil drilling, logging, and mining in national forests and coastal areas.[22] A combination of regulatory and legislative changes, begun in the 1970s but accelerated under Reagan, permitted savings and loan institutions to vastly expand their lending practices for both single-family homes and risky commercial real estate. To help automobile manufacturers save money, they were permitted to reduce the safety margins on items like bumpers.

All of these actions increased corporate profitability and some, like airline and communications deregulation, improved options for consumers. But others came at a steep cost to the environment, to worker safety, and to taxpayers. The most costly deregulation, that of the savings and loan (S&L) industry, initially spurred a construction boom. After 1982, S&Ls were allowed to expand their lending from the modestly profitable, but safe, home mortgage business to the potentially lucrative, but risky, commercial real estate market. With little regulatory oversight, S&Ls made massive gambles, and when the bubble burst in 1989–90, taxpayers had to bail out these banks at a cost of several hundred billion dollars.

Reagan justified "unleashing market forces" by noting that for twenty years, America had fought a war on poverty, "and poverty won." Government red tape and scams (he often spoke of a mythical "welfare queen" who used dozens of aliases to collect a small fortune), the president claimed, had undermined efforts to help the poor.

Although the poverty rate of about 13 percent had barely budged since Lyndon Johnson called for a war on poverty in 1965, the demography of poverty had changed dramatically. Before 1965, the poor were most often elderly, sick Americans. But passage of Medicare (which Reagan opposed) and the expansion of Social Security had greatly reduced the number of elderly poor. By 1981 the typical Americans living in poverty were a single mother and her young children. This "feminization of poverty," as some called it, showed that although targeted social spending could alleviate some suffering, many problems remained.

To be sure, total family income rose a bit during the 1980s. This was not because average Americans earned more. Wages actually stagnated. Rather, in most households, wives and young mothers joined the work-force to make ends meet. The Reagan era's big winners were the very wealthy. Wall Street traders and real estate moguls such as Carl Icahn, T. Boone Pickens, Ivan Boesky, Michael Milken and Donald Trump made hundreds of millions of dollars annually in dubious deals that relied on borrowed money often secured by risky "junk bonds." Boesky spoke for many of the super-wealthy when he boasted to graduating business majors at the University of

California, Berkeley, in 1986, that "greed is healthy." (Oliver Stone appropriated the phrase for his 1987 film *Wall Street*, itself a clear indictment of the super-wealthy.) Greed was certainly good for Boesky—until he went to jail for insider stock trading. In aggregate, the wealthiest 1 percent of Americans saw their share of national income nearly double in the 1980s, from 8.1 percent to 15 percent.

The Reagan years witnessed deregulation beyond the economic sphere. Like many conservatives, Reagan believed that, since the 1950s, "activist" federal judges, especially on the Supreme Court, had overstepped their role. Instead of interpreting the law, they "legislated from the bench." Their misguided concerns with the rights of accused criminals, victims of racial or gender discrimination, or those who opposed official aid to religion, conservatives maintained, undermined public morals and distorted what they believed to be the original intent of the constitution.

Reagan was certainly not a racist in the narrow sense of the term. He believed in equal opportunity and opposed racial discrimination. Reagan recalled how in high school, he had played football with African Americans, and how his mother had taken in a visiting black athlete who could not find a hotel room. But aside from these long-ago personal kindnesses, he showed little understanding about the legacy of racism in America or the toll it continued to take. With the end of formal racial barriers, Reagan insisted, government's duty ceased. Additional efforts on behalf of minorities, such as affirmative action programs, represented "reverse discrimination" against whites. Speaking to white Southerners, Reagan spoke openly of his support for "states' rights," a phrase which many interpreted as coded language critical of civil rights.

As a private citizen in 1964, Reagan opposed the landmark Civil Rights Act as an infringement on property and states' rights. He condemned the 1965 Voting Rights Act, which opened the polls to African Americans in the South as "insulting to Southerners." As a presidential candidate, Reagan spoke against school busing for racial balance and criticized efforts to enact a holiday in honor of Dr. Martin Luther King, Jr.[23] He also favored the restoration of tax benefits to private segregated Christian schools.

His tenets had sway. Under Reagan, the Justice Department tried to restore tax breaks (disallowed by Jimmy Carter) for all-white private schools, often called Christian academies, which had opened mainly in the South when public schools were integrated in the 1970s. The department questioned the legality of many affirmative action programs, opposed extension of the landmark 1965 Voting Rights Act (although Reagan signed a Congressional bill extending it), and appointed members of the Equal Employment Opportunity Commission, who, like Clarence Thomas—a future Supreme Court justice—refused to act on most claims of discrimination brought forward by women and minorities. In 1988, at the end of his presidency, Reagan vetoed the Civil Rights Restoration Act (designed to block discrimination against women and minorities in federally funded programs), only to have Congressional Republicans join Democrats in overriding his action.

As president, Reagan had the opportunity to appoint nearly 400 federal judges—a majority of the total—as well as Chief Justice of the Supreme Court William Rehnquist and three associate justices, Sandra Day O'Connor (the first woman on the high court), Antonin Scalia, and Anthony Kennedy. These appointments moved the federal judiciary in a distinctly more conservative direction and influenced rulings long after Reagan's departure. Rulings in the late 1980s limited protection for criminal defendants, upheld most state death penalty laws, and made it harder for women, minorities, the elderly, and the disabled to sue employers for employment discrimination. Other court rulings restricted but did not eliminate abortions.

Reagan and the Justice Department encouraged Congress and state legislatures to enact stiff mandatory sentencing laws, especially for repeat felons and drug users. In 1980 state prisons held about 300,000 inmates and federal prisons about 25,000. A decade later, the combined total exceeded 800,000, making the United States the leader among industrial nations in rates of incarceration. The boom in prison construction and jobs for guards was sometimes dubbed Reagan's housing and employment program, while other critics spoke of an emerging "prison–industrial complex."

Efforts to impose harsh sentences on criminals coincided with a federal war on drugs that Reagan ramped up in the mid-1980s. The president and first lady initiated what they called the "Just Say NO" campaign to discourage drug use. Popular anxiety over this perennial problem increased, along with the violence associated with the appearance of "crack" cocaine. The relative risks of drug use were seldom discussed in a way that put them into perspective. On average during the 1980s, "only" about 5,000 people died annually from illegal drug overdoses. More died from drug-related violence. In comparison, at least 10,000 Americans died annually from reactions to over-the-counter medications. Public health authorities attributed several hundred thousand deaths annually to alcohol and tobacco use. Nevertheless, by the time Reagan left office, federal and state authorities were spending about $10 billion annually on the drug war, mostly for police and prisons, not prevention or treatment. Some 750,000

Americans were arrested each year for drug offenses, most commonly involving marijuana. A disproportionate number of those convicted were black or Latino. As in earlier and later decades, rates of drug use fluctuated with little regard to criminal sanctions.

Reagan, with the assistance of congressional allies, promoted a conservative sexual agenda. They reduced funding to international population control agencies that promoted birth control or even mentioned abortion, endorsed a constitutional ban on abortion, and sponsored "chastity clinics" for teens. These stressed abstinence from sex as the only safe and permissible form of birth control.

The president spoke reverently of the "traditional family," which resembled the cast of a 1950s television sitcom. As a divorced man who had distant relationships with his children, it certainly did not resemble *his* family. In 1981 a majority of women worked outside the home, about 40 percent of marriages ended in divorce, a growing number of unmarried couples lived together, and at least one-third of children were born to unmarried mothers. Nonetheless, Reagan's homilies about tradition changed very little.

Early in the decade, the appearance of AIDS (acquired immune deficiency syndrome) created a health crisis with strong sexual overtones. The result of the human immunodeficiency virus (HIV, identified in 1984), which destroyed the immune system, AIDS caused a vulnerability to many infections. The disease likely originated in Africa decades earlier and spread slowly. HIV was transmitted through the exchange of bodily fluids. Transmission was most common among gay men, intravenous drug users, and their partners.

The spread of AIDS coincided with the growth of the gay consciousness and rights movements. This prompted a reaction from some conservatives, such as Reagan adviser Patrick Buchanan, who dubbed it the "Gay Plague." By the late 1980s, about 50,000 Americans had died of AIDS and as many as 1 million carried HIV.

Reagan was silent on the subject until 1985, the year his friend and closeted gay actor Rock Hudson died of AIDS. The president then appointed an advisory panel, led by Surgeon General C. Everett Koop, which issued a call for more federal research dollars and a campaign to encourage sexually active Americans to use condoms to avoid infection. Reagan expressed compassion for those suffering from AIDS and told Americans not to be afraid to donate blood, but refused to endorse condom use or discuss the subject further.

Koop, whom Reagan appointed as the nation's chief medical officer largely because of his opposition to abortion, emerged as the administration's unlikely hero on the AIDS crisis and other public health issues. The surgeon general's dramatic beard and stern visage gave him the appearance of an Old Testament prophet. To Reagan's surprise, as well as that of skeptical Democrats who had opposed his selection, Koop insisted that as a public health official he must go beyond his personal morality and speak forcefully about how safe sex could reduce the risk of transmitting HIV.

Koop also ignored Reagan's call to reduce federal regulations when he energized federal efforts, begun in the 1960s, to drive down smoking rates.[24] In a series of high-profile reports, Koop condemned cigarette smoking as the nation's "chief preventable cause of death," compared nicotine addiction to heroin use, and urged stronger state and federal efforts, such as banning smoking in public areas, to make America a "smoke-free society" by the year 2000.

By the end of his first term, Reagan had trimmed social spending at the margins but came nowhere near his professed goal of rolling back major Great Society programs like Medicare, Medicaid, Food Stamps, and federal support for public broadcasting and the arts. This bothered only a small number of hardcore conservatives. Most Americans were impressed by Reagan's sunny disposition, resolve, and the sense he conveyed that things had greatly improved since the gloomy Carter years. Even if they did not always agree with what he advocated, the public liked the fact that Reagan stood for something.

In 1982, when the recession peaked, Democrats and media pundits predicted Reagan would be a one-term president. By 1984, however, inflation was tamed, employment had grown, oil prices had fallen, and federal tax cuts had provided working- and middle-class Americans a few more dollars in their pockets. Most people also believed their nation enjoyed greater security and international respect. Reagan's popularity soared and dashed Democratic hopes that he might be voted out of office.

A large majority of Americans embraced Reagan's reelection slogan (based on a car advertisement)—it was again "Morning in America." Democrats, who sputtered about the unfairness of tax cuts for the rich and the ballooning deficit, hardly laid a glove on Reagan. In November he swept to victory, winning forty-nine states against challenger and former vice president Walter Mondale. When asked what he hoped to accomplish in his second term, Reagan beamed, "Let's do it all!"

In fact, Reagan undertook few new domestic initiatives. Between 1985 and 1988, Congress passed only two significant pieces of domestic legislation that he backed enthusiastically. These included a tax reform bill drafted by the Treasury Department and modified by Democrats in Congress that closed many loopholes exploited by the rich. Because the bill reduced the number of tax brackets from fourteen to three, Reagan called it a step toward a "flat rate" income tax that some libertarians favored. In practice, the 1986 law shifted a bit more of the tax burden back to the wealthy, who had benefited from Reagan's 1981 tax cuts. Also with Reagan's support, Congressional Democrats took the lead in passing the Simpson-Rodino immigration act in 1986. The law substantially raised the number of people allowed to immigrate legally and, much to the dismay of some conservatives, offered amnesty to millions of undocumented migrants living in the United States.

After Reagan coasted to victory in 1984, neither the president nor his supporters guessed that his second term would be dominated by his deep involvement in a foreign policy scandal—the Iran-Contra affair—and the dramatic improvement of relations between the United States and the Soviet Union.

4

Confronting the Soviet Union/
Ending the Cold War

℃

Reagan was praised as much for his foreign policy achievements as for anything he did at home. To many Americans his ardent celebration of patriotism and military
fortitude, resistance to communism, and tough words
for terrorists not only made the nation safer but, in the
words of Reagan's close friend British Prime Minister
Margaret Thatcher, won the Cold War "without firing
a shot." Upon Reagan's death in June 2004, Republican
leaders such as Texas Congressman Tom DeLay praised
him as an "intellectual warrior" who "marshaled ideas like
troops" and freed the world from the threat of communism. Another funeral orator asserted that when Reagan
became president in 1981, the Soviets and their proxies

were winning the Cold War, but by the time he left office, the Soviets had been tamed and put on the fast track to the ash heap of history.

Reagan's powerful antipathy toward communism seemed exemplified by a gaffe he made in August 1984. Just before giving a radio address, he spoke some unscripted words into a microphone that had been mistakenly activated. "My fellow Americans," Reagan declared, "I'm pleased to tell you today I've signed legislation that will outlaw the Soviet Union forever. We begin bombing in five minutes." Although he quickly apologized for the remark, conservatives saw it as evidence of his true grit, whereas liberals voiced astonishment at his casual talk of nuclear war. Seven years later, when Soviet leader Mikhail Gorbachev actually signed a decree dissolving the Soviet state, many looked back at Reagan as prescient.

Shortly before Reagan left office in 1989, Robert MacFarlane, the third of Reagan's six national security advisers, wrote to his former boss that the transformation of the Soviet system represented a "vindication of your seven-year strategy." Confronted by the "renewal" of American economic, military, and spiritual power, Soviet leaders understood that "they simply had to change their system or face inevitable decline."[25] Reagan, MacFarlane and others asserted, made the defeat, rather than the containment, of communism a priority. From

Truman to Carter, presidents of both parties valued stability over confrontation and sought to make deals with the Kremlin. Reagan considered communism both a moral evil and an inherent threat to peace. By both talking and acting tough, and by rearming America, Reagan has been credited by his supporters with "winning the Cold War."

Without question, Reagan expanded U.S. military power and restored public confidence in presidential leadership. His rhetoric uplifted the spirits of Americans—and many foreigners—who had considered themselves victims in an unfriendly world of hostage-taking, nuclear threats, rising oil prices, and Third World insurgencies. Yet, as in his domestic policy, a gulf often existed between the idealism, self-assurance, and occasional bluster of Reagan's calls to action and his administration's actual accomplishments.

Reagan oversaw the largest military buildup in peacetime history—spending increased from about $157 billion in 1981 to $253 billion in 1985 and $304 billion in 1989. He also played a critical role, especially in his final years in office, in transforming the Soviet–American relationship. But proof that doubling arms spending, talking tough, and intervening in Central America, Africa, and the Middle East changed Soviet policy remains elusive. Many of the covert military operations Reagan approved had unintended and sometimes dire consequences. For example, the Central Intelligence Agency's (CIA) arming of Islamic guerrillas resisting Soviet forces in Afghanistan contributed to the Red Army's withdrawal. But U.S. aid also promoted the arming and rise of an Islamist terror network in that country and neighboring Pakistan.

Reagan agreed with the argument made by Jeane Kirkpatrick (whom he named ambassador to the United Nations) that the United States should support pro-American dictatorships in the Third World as necessary barriers to communism. For much of his presidency, Reagan stood by tyrants such as Ferdinand Marcos in the Philippines, Jean-Claude Duvalier in Haiti, and the white supremacist regime in South Africa, even when they were challenged by noncommunist uprisings. In light of two wars later fought in Iraq, in 1991 and from 2003 onward, it is startling to recall the support provided by the Reagan administration to Saddam Hussein during the 1980s, despite the dictator's brutal reign and his use of poison gas against both his own population and Iranian troops engaged in a war with Iraq.

As candidate and as president, Reagan spoke forcefully about the division he saw between the peaceful democratic world led by the United States and the aggressive web of communist dictatorships controlled by Moscow. In 1980 and often thereafter he remarked that the Soviet Union "underlies all the unrest that is going on" in the world. If "they weren't engaged in this game of dominos, there wouldn't be any hotspots in the world."[26] Reagan stressed his religious antipathy for communism in an address to the National Association of Evangelicals on March 8, 1983. The Soviet Union, he declared, was "the focus of evil in the modern world," truly an "evil empire."[27]

Reagan held what he saw as a simple truth: the Soviet Union was doomed to fall. In addressing the British Parliament in June 1982, the president dismissed the Soviet Union as a force that "runs against the tide of history." With communism's economic, political, and social systems all "astounding" failures, Reagan consigned communism to the "ash heap of history." Although Reagan's perception of the Soviet Union might be "primitive," as CIA Deputy Director Robert Gates acknowledged, his clarity of vision allowed him to see the future in ways that eluded more sophisticated thinkers.

Reagan attributed American vulnerability to its failure to win the Vietnam War. The resulting "Vietnam syndrome," an unwillingness to use force to resist Soviet pressure or to defend foreign friends and interests, explained why American diplomats in 1979 had been seized as hostages in Iran while Soviet troops occupied Afghanistan and Moscow-backed insurgents made a play for power in Central America and Africa. As a first step toward restoring national resolve, he told a gathering of Vietnam-era veterans in 1980, Americans must "recognize that ours, in truth, was a noble cause." Alexander Haig, whom the newly elected Reagan named secretary of state in 1981, echoed this theme, proclaiming that the American people would henceforth "shed their sackcloth and ashes." Taking a cue from the president's call in his inaugural address to "dream heroic dreams," the new administration pledged to restore the nation's military superiority, defend allies, and, in what was later informally called the "Reagan doctrine," assist anticommunist movements throughout the world. Not by chance, the president's aides explained, did Iran release its long-held American captives just as Reagan took the presidential oath on January 20, 1981.

During his first term, Reagan utilized tough rhetoric, heavy arms spending, trade sanctions, and covert interventions to bolster pro-American elements in the Third World and confront perceived Soviet challenges. Yet in most cases, including Lebanon, Nicaragua, Angola, and Mozambique, U.S.-backed forces failed to achieve their goals. In Afghanistan, CIA-supported mujahideen (Islamist guerrillas) eventually drove out Soviet invaders but did so at a steep cost. Many of the militants in Afghanistan and Pakistan formed the core of what later became both the

Taliban and Osama bin Laden's al-Qaeda movements. To ensure Pakistan's help in supplying the mujahideen, Washington backed that nation's military regime and tacitly supported its drive to acquire nuclear weapons. Reagan's personal determination to fund the anticommunist rebels in Nicaragua, despite Congress's ban on aid, prompted his illegal arms sales to Iran as well as the arms-for-hostage debacle known as Iran-Contra, which became public at the end of 1986.

In contrast to these dubious ventures, Reagan achieved a major success in his effort to promote democracy in Poland. After the imposition, in July 1981, of martial law and banning of the Solidarity movement, which challenged the Communist monopoly on power, Reagan directed the CIA to work closely with the Vatican and Polish Catholic Church to assist Solidarity members in and out of jail in continuing their political campaign. This support helped sustain democratic forces. Along with eventual changes in Soviet policy, it undermined Communist control in Poland and elsewhere in Eastern Europe.

At a time when several European leaders distanced themselves from Washington, Reagan forged so close a personal bond with British Prime Minister Margaret Thatcher that the two leaders jokingly called each other "soul mates." The Conservative Party leader took office in 1979, promising to revive Britain's sagging economy

and self-image. Thatcher privatized state-owned indus-
tries, curbed the power of labor unions, and expanded
military spending. These policies endeared her to Reagan.
Both leaders promoted free markets as a global economic
model and anticommunism as a basic foreign policy.

Reagan's friendship gave Thatcher more clout in
European affairs than she would have otherwise enjoyed.
The president sided with Great Britain in 1982 when it
fought a brief war to drive Argentine forces out of the
British colony on the Falkland Islands in the South Atlan-
tic. In turn, Thatcher's spirited defense of Reagan's more
confrontational policies, such as the deployment of medi-
um-range missiles, provided a veneer of international support. Thatcher permitted the United States to base several
hundred new atomic-armed cruise missiles, aimed at the
Soviet Union, on British soil in the mid-1980s.

Like presidents before him, Reagan inherited an unsta-
ble, violent Middle East and left the region in pretty much
the same condition. Conflicts between Israelis and Pales-
tinians, among Lebanese factions, within Afghanistan, and
between Iraq and Iran continued throughout the 1980s.
This violence, along with America's continued strong support for Israel, set the stage for future problems, some
involving terrorism aimed at the United States.

In the early 1980s Lebanese religious and political
factions resumed their periodic civil slaughter, with Israel

and Syria backing armed groups. When some presidential aides criticized Secretary of State Haig's June 1982 support for an Israeli invasion of Lebanon, Haig quit in a huff. George Shultz, the more thoughtful and nuanced diplomat named as Haig's successor, had no more success in stabilizing the area.

As chaos engulfed Lebanon, Reagan dispatched marines to join French and Italian troops as peacekeepers. Once there, the marines assisted Christian militias fighting Muslim forces backed by Syria. In response, on April 18, 1983, a suicide squad blew up the U.S. embassy in Beirut, killing sixty-three people. United States Navy ships off the Lebanese coast then bombarded several Islamic militia strongholds. On October 23, Muslim fighters retaliated by driving a truck filled with explosives into a U.S. Marine barracks near the Beirut airport, killing 241 men.

Reagan offered a stirring tribute to the fallen marines but no credible explanation of their mission or the reason for their deaths. A few months later, in his 1984 State of the Union message, he described the marine presence as "central to our credibility on a global scale." Two weeks later, without explanation, he withdrew American forces from Beirut.

Public reaction to the disaster in Beirut was muted in part because of the lavish media attention focused on a simultaneous crisis in Grenada, a tiny Caribbean island.

Although Grenada had been ruled by Marxists since 1979, neither the Carter nor the Reagan administration had paid much attention to it. The only American presence consisted of about 500 students enrolled in a private medical college.

As a contingent of armed Cuban construction workers labored on an airport designed either to boost tourism (as Grenada claimed) or to serve as a Soviet-Cuban air base (as Washington asserted), a more militant Marxist faction seized control of Grenada on October 12, 1983. Immediately after the October 23 catastrophe in Beirut, Reagan declared that the American students on Grenada might become hostages, although none had been threatened. On October 25 he ordered thousands of marines and army troops to liberate Grenada and the American students from a "brutal gang of thugs."

The invasion force quickly secured the island. The students flew home, and a photograph of one of them kissing American soil became a staple in the president's reelection commercials. As if to compensate for the Beirut debacle, the Pentagon awarded an unprecedented 8,000 medals to members of the assault force. Free elections restored representative government to the island. Most Americans approved of the operation, telling pollsters they were pleased that the United States had "won one for a change." News coverage of the invasion alerted many Americans to

Grenada's lovely beaches and eventually sparked a tourist boom, facilitated by the Cuban-built airport.

Despite the muddle in places like Beirut, many conservatives insist that Reagan had a "secret" plan to bankrupt the Soviets by cutting off their access to Western loans and technology and by launching an expensive arms race Moscow could not afford. Reagan's enthusiastic promotion of his Strategic Defense Initiative (SDI) antimissile plan ("Star Wars"), revealed in 1983, is cited as an example of this strategy to force the Soviets into a high-technology competition designed to break the back of their creaky economy.

Assertions that Reagan's multipronged assault forced a virtual Soviet surrender and the subsequent demise of communism have an appealing ring but do not conform closely to actual events. In 1980 Jimmy Carter had already stopped most U.S. exports to the Soviet Union in order to punish Moscow for its Afghan incursion. Upon taking office in 1981, Reagan *restored* agricultural sales—the major U.S. trade item with the Soviets. He did pressure America's Japanese and European allies to cease their technology sales to the Soviet Union. This ban lasted for about three years, before Washington bowed to allied complaints and relaxed trade sanctions. Since the easing occurred *before* major changes took place in Soviet policy, it appears that economic sanctions did not force a Soviet retreat.

Nor is there much evidence that the surge in U.S. military spending between 1981 and 1985 intimidated the Soviets. Moscow had invested heavily in new armaments during the last half of the 1970s and scaled back the pace of military production in the early 1980s for a variety of reasons unrelated to Reagan's challenge. Nevertheless, Reagan and his top advisers asserted in public and in private that Soviet military strength continued to expand. They acknowledged that the communist economic system was badly stressed but thought it would probably muddle along for several decades.

Ironically, the Soviet economy was much weaker than U.S. intelligence analysts or Reagan estimated. The country suffered from a variety of social afflictions, such as a low birth rate, declining longevity rates, and high rates of chronic alcoholism, in addition to badly mismanaged agricultural and industrial sectors. Soviet technology lagged far behind that of the United States, Western Europe, and Japan. Part of the Soviet leadership's determination to maintain their nation's isolation stemmed from a desire to keep these vulnerabilities hidden from outsiders and to keep information about the outside world off-limits to Soviet citizens. Assertions by some of Reagan's aides that they—and he—had secretly known and exploited this vulnerability were largely after-the-fact explanations.[28]

Reagan's proposed laser-powered space-based missile shield, announced in a speech in March 1983, troubled Soviet leaders, but not for the reasons the president imagined. (He expected it to render their nuclear missiles impotent and obsolete.) Soviet strategists never thought SDI would be very effective, but worried that it might work as a backup if the United States launched a preemptive strike that knocked out most Soviet missiles before their launch. In that case, even a leaky defense could pick off the few retaliatory missiles the Soviets would fire. Thus, Soviet strategists considered SDI more as an offensive system than a defensive one.

Some hard-liners around Reagan had exactly this strategy in mind. Other advisers considered SDI less of a viable weapon than a useful bargaining chip to pressure the Soviets. Reagan, as his private words reveal, harbored a sensible and genuine fear of nuclear weapons. He probably believed that SDI, if built, could protect American lives. This would provide the president with an alternative to the strategy of deterrence, which relied on the threat of mutual assured destruction, or MAD, to keep the peace. Reagan seemed puzzled when domestic and foreign critics questioned his motives or his promise eventually to share SDI technology even with the Soviet Union.[29]

Although SDI remained a concept, not a reality, Reagan insisted, and many of his supporters agree, that it forced a change in Soviet behavior.[30] In fact, rather than bring the Soviets to the negotiating table, Reagan's advocacy of SDI may have played into the hands of Soviet hard-liners before 1985 and delayed the decision by Soviet reformers after 1985 to resume arms control talks with Washington. Only at the end of 1986, when Soviet scientists concluded that a space shield posed no offensive threat and was unlikely to be built, did the nation's leadership push for improved relations with the United States.

Historians generally avoid attributing fundamental historical shifts to a single cause. Nevertheless, the critical variable in ending the Cold War was most likely the selection in 1985 by aging Communist Party officials of the 54-year-old Mikhail Gorbachev as the party and national leader. As the best-educated, most widely traveled, and most personable Soviet chief since Vladimir Lenin, Gorbachev charmed foreign leaders and presented a far different face to the world than had the succession of aging oligarchs who ruled the country since the 1970s.

Partly because of his intelligence and travels abroad, Gorbachev recognized the inherent weakness of the Soviet system. In some important ways he shared Reagan's critique of the inefficient and undemocratic structure over which he presided. In the past, Soviet leaders had solved economic problems by simply ordering collective farms to produce more grain or miners to extract more coal. But these methods not only paid diminishing returns but were especially ill suited to promoting the kinds of technological innovation that spurred advances in the production of both defense and consumer goods. Faced with technological obsolescence and a restive population at home and in Eastern Europe that was becoming increasingly aware of its relative backwardness, the Soviet Union was likely to slip further behind the rest of the industrialized world. Gorbachev sought to save and revive the system through democratic political and market reforms. Under his leadership, the Soviet Union did not so much "lose" the arms race and Cold War as call them off. Moreover, this change coincided with Reagan's need to recover from a humiliating scandal of his own making.

From the beginning of his presidency, Reagan and his closest aides perceived a Soviet and Cuban threat to the Western Hemisphere. They articulated fears that seemed lifted from the early Cold War. Reagan and his national security team spoke menacingly of a "Moscow–Havana" axis whose Soviet-armed Cuban agents conspired to spread revolution in both Africa and Latin America.

As a candidate in 1980, Reagan had bitterly criticized the Carter administration for abandoning the Nicaraguan dictator Anastasio Somoza, whose family had ruled the country since the 1930s. Once elected, Reagan warned that the leftist Sandinista movement, which had toppled

Somoza, would turn Nicaragua into a Soviet outpost and a "safe house and command post for international terror," if it had not already done so.

In spite of Reagan's passion, the public seemed apathetic. When it came to Latin America, pollsters found that the public scarcely noted or cared who ruled in Tegucigalpa or Managua. At the same time, they deferred to Reagan as long as Americans were not killed in combat. As a result, the administration focused on supplying military aid to friendly governments in the region and supporting covert warfare that placed few American lives at risk. For example, during the 1980s, Reagan requested and Congress authorized spending nearly $5 billion to bolster the government of tiny El Salvador, a nominal democracy dominated by hard-line militarists that had been battling a left-wing rebellion since 1979. Congress placed a cap on the number of U.S. military advisers in El Salvador but otherwise asked few questions.

Reagan's policy toward Nicaragua proved far more controversial. Nothing he did in his eight years as president tarnished his reputation or called into question his judgment as seriously as did his decision to sell weapons to Iran as part of a scheme both to ransom U.S. hostages in Beirut and to fund anticommunist fighters in Central America.

Nicaragua's Sandinista leaders were, as Reagan asserted, genuine Marxists who disliked the United States, blocked free elections, received aid from Cuba and the Soviet Union, and provided at least some support to other leftist groups in Central America. But Sandinista abuses hardly matched the brutality inflicted on civilians by pro–United States regimes in nearby El Salvador, Guatemala, and Honduras. In any case, tiny Nicaragua, with fewer inhabitants than many American cities, hardly seemed an existential threat to the hemisphere.

In 1981 Reagan ordered CIA director William Casey to bolster a small anti-Sandinista force called the *contrarevolucionarios*, or Contras. (Argentina's military regime, an early patron of the Contras, dropped out when Reagan supported British military action to retake the Falkland Islands.) The president described these guerrillas as "freedom fighters" and "the moral equal of our Founding Fathers." Over the next few years Contra ranks swelled to over ten thousand men. Most Contra leaders were veterans of the old Somoza dictatorship.

In December 1981 Reagan signed a secret order authorizing Contra aid for the purpose of deposing the Sandinistas. In 1982, when reports surfaced linking Contra attacks to thousands of civilian deaths in Nicaragua, Congress passed a resolution named for Representative Edward P. Boland that capped CIA assistance to the rebels at $24 million and ordered that none of the funds be used to topple the Nicaraguan government.

In October 1984, after learning that the CIA and Contras had illegally mined Nicaraguan harbors, Congress, with the tacit support of many Republicans, including Senator Barry Goldwater, passed a stricter version of the Boland law that barred any U.S. government funds from going to the Contras for any purpose.

These restrictions infuriated Reagan, who ridiculed Congress as a committee of busybodies. He told National Security Adviser Robert McFarlane and his deputy Admiral John Poindexter as well as the National Security Council (NSC) staffer Lieutenant Colonel Oliver North "to do whatever you have to do to help these people [the Contras] keep body and soul together."[31] For a president who seldom issued clear instructions to subordinates, this was a definitive order.

McFarlane, Poindexter, and North devised a scheme to "privatize" Contra aid by soliciting funds from wealthy foreign governments, like Brunei and Saudi Arabia, and rich American conservatives, such as brewer Joseph Coors, a friend of Reagan's. The donations paid for weapons supplied to the guerrillas. (In appreciation, the Contras placed a "Coors" beer logo on one of their aircraft.) The president did not know all the details, but McFarlane and Poindexter, McFarlane's successor as national security adviser, kept him closely informed of their activities and received his blessing.

During 1985 Contra aid merged with secret and illegal contacts with Iran. Reagan had publicly condemned the Iranian regime as an "outlaw state." He had previously sent Donald Rumsfeld, then a corporate executive and Pentagon consultant, as an emissary to Baghdad to assure Saddam Hussein of U.S. support in Iraq's costly war with Iran. American strategists actually hoped to prevent an all-out victory by either side and at various times supplied aid to both Iraq and Iran. United States law barred providing Iran any military equipment unless the president informed Congress in writing of a compelling reason to do so. Reagan found a reason but declined to notify anyone.

For several years Reagan had been upset by the plight of seven Americans who had been kidnapped in Beirut and held hostage by Islamic militias linked to Iran. With the exception of one hostage, CIA agent William Buckley, all were private citizens who had remained in Lebanon despite official warnings. Recalling the public outcry over Carter's failure to rescue Americans held hostage in Iran, Reagan moved to break the deadlock. In mid-1985 an Iranian businessman contacted McFarlane and claimed that he could secure the hostages' release in return for U.S. arms sales to "moderate" elements in Iran who might take power following the death of supreme leader Ayatollah Khomeini.

Despite his public pledge "never to negotiate with terrorists," Reagan told McFarlane, "Gee, that sounds pretty good." In a diary entry of August 14, 1985, the president indicated he liked the idea of making a deal to free "our seven kidnap victims." He said nothing about building a new relationship with Iran. Over the next year Reagan authorized several secret arms sales to Iran. Although three hostages were eventually released, three more were taken as replacements. In effect, the arms sales created a market for hostage-taking.

This ill-conceived scheme took an even more bizarre turn when the NSC's Colonel North came up with what he called a "neat idea": overcharging the Iranians for American weapons and using the profits to support the Nicaraguan Contras. As North joked, the Iranians would unknowingly make a "Contra-bution." This violated federal law, since profits from any sale of U.S. government property had to be returned to the U.S. Treasury, not given to the president's pet guerrilla charity in defiance of Congress's specific ban on funding the Contras.

The web unraveled in October 1986, when Sandinista gunners shot down a CIA-chartered plane carrying weapons to the Contras. A surviving American crew member divulged details of the secret aid program. In November, Iran revealed that the illegal arms shipments had not gone to "moderates" but to loyalists of Khomeini, the Iranian religious leader most reviled by Americans for his role in seizing hostages in 1979. Reagan and his aides had been played for fools.

Reagan, Casey, North, and other participants tried to cover up the scandal by shredding documents and lying about their actions to the press, to Congress, to a special prosecutor, and to the American public. Despite evidence of his participation, Reagan insisted he knew nothing about any arms-for-hostages deal or illegal funding of the Contras. The public did not believe him, and in early 1987 Reagan's approval rating fell to 47 percent. Under tremendous pressure to come clean, the president appointed a blue-ribbon inquiry panel chaired by former senator John Tower. After hearing misleading and confused testimony from Reagan and others, the Tower commission concluded in its February 1987 report that the Iran arms sales had devolved into a sordid ransom scheme designed to fund the Contras illegally. Reagan's actions ran "directly counter" to his public promise to punish terrorists. The report portrayed the president as disengaged, uninformed, and easily manipulated, but not a felon.

Reagan sidestepped the criticism by firing several of his aides linked to the scandal and giving a speech on March 4, 1987, in which he appeared to accept responsibility without actually doing so. The "facts" might suggest he permitted ransom payments and other illegal acts,

Reagan asserted, but in his "heart" he never meant to break the law. Congressional probes and criminal trials over the next few years added many details to the Iran-Contra episode. After Reagan left office, several participants, including North and McFarlane, confirmed that the president had approved their actions and had blocked a full investigation.[32]

Despite talk among Democrats of impeachment (they had retaken control of the Senate in November 1986), Reagan prevailed, retaining an important quotient of good will from the public. The competing investigations into Iran-Contra often lacked focus. But perhaps the most important reason why the scandal faded was the dramatic improvement in Soviet–American relations. Since 1985 a thaw had begun between Moscow and Washington. By 1987 fundamental changes had occurred inside the Soviet Union, and Reagan rushed to embrace them. Ironically, improved relations with the "evil empire" helped salvage Reagan's presidency.

To his credit, Reagan possessed the flexibility and good sense to respond positively to Gorbachev's reforms in the Soviet Union and his calls for international cooperation. For over a year after Gorbachev assumed power in March 1985, Reagan's hard-line advisers convinced him to reject overtures to or from the new Soviet chief. One aide even gave the president a doll that depicted Gorbachev as "Darth Vader," the villain of the popular *Star Wars* films. But the Iran-Contra scandal had discredited most of those aides. Secretary of State George Shultz, a moderate who had opposed Iran-Contra and favored resuming arms control talks with the Soviet Union, emerged as the president's most trusted foreign policy advisor.

Since 1981, Reagan had refused to meet with Soviet leaders, deflecting critics first by saying the United States must first rearm and then with the quip "They keep dying on me."[33] (Between 1982 and 1985, Soviet leaders Leonid Brezhnev, Yuri Andropov, and Konstantin Chernenko died in office.) But even when signs emerged during 1985 that Gorbachev represented a dramatic break with the Soviet past, Reagan hesitated to talk to him.

Four women whom Reagan admired, none of them U.S. officials, altered his outlook. After meeting Gorbachev, Margaret Thatcher informed Reagan that she found him charming and someone with whom "we could do business." Nancy Reagan later said she told her husband that in a "dangerous world" it was "ridiculous for the two heavily armed superpowers to be sitting there and not talking to each other." Sensing that he needed some outside encouragement to change his approach, she arranged for astrologer Joan Quigley, a family favorite, to tell the president that based on the stars, Gorbachev's "Aquarian planet is in such harmony with Ronnie's...they'll share a vision." Suzanne Massie, an author of popular books on Russian culture who Reagan consulted privately, also urged that he meet the new Soviet leader.[34]

In November 1985 Reagan and Gorbachev met and talked for several hours at a villa on the shore of Lake Geneva in Switzerland. Although they skirted most issues of substance, each made a favorable impression on the other. Reagan found Gorbachev far more thoughtful and flexible than he anticipated. He entertained the Soviet leader by telling stories about glamorous Hollywood celebrities. Gorbachev found Reagan's warmth and informality appealing, quite unlike the "caveman" he expected to encounter.

The two met again at Reykjavik, Iceland, in October 1986. Each broached bold ideas for cutting the number of nuclear weapons. But progress halted when Reagan insisted that the United States must be free to deploy a space-based antimissile system no matter what. Gorbachev retorted that if all the nuclear-armed nations made substantial cuts in their weapons, the United States could not be permitted to deploy SDI and thereby nullify the small, remaining Soviet nuclear deterrent. Reagan left in a huff, giving the impression that the meeting had failed. However, both leaders had revealed a genuine desire to ratchet down their nuclear arsenals dramatically and to seek cooperation on a range of issues.

After Reykjavik, Soviet scientists persuaded Gorbachev that SDI would not be operational for decades, if ever. This assurance—and not Reagan's refusal to back away from SDI—encouraged Gorbachev to propose missile cuts without insisting on an SDI ban. At the same time, Gorbachev recognized that his effort to revitalize the Soviet economy and promote democratic reform could not be achieved without reducing military spending and seeking economic cooperation with the United States, Western Europe, and Japan.

During 1987 Reagan became convinced that Gorbachev's domestic reforms and calls for international cooperation were not just clever tactics, as some White House skeptics argued, but revealed a sincere desire to remake both the Soviet Union and its relationship with the world. Reagan must also have recognized that improved Soviet–American relations would restore his own stature, which had been so badly tarnished by the Iran-Contra scandal. In place of his earlier condemnation of "godless communism" and the "evil empire," the president described his new approach toward the Soviet Union as "trust, but verify."

That June, Reagan spoke to a crowd at Berlin's Brandenburg Gate, not far from where President John F. Kennedy, twenty-five years before, had so memorably condemned the construction of the Berlin Wall. Pointing to the stark Cold War symbol, Reagan declared, "Mr. Gorbachev, tear down this wall!" Many considered this evidence that Reagan still deeply mistrusted the Soviet leader. (The speech took on added symbolism when, in November 1989, exuberant Germans did just what Reagan had urged Gorbachev to do, tearing down the wall with sledgehammers, chisels, and any other tools they could get their hands on. Soviet forces still in East Germany refused to prop up the Communist regime.) However, Reagan seems to have had other motives, such as placating hard-liners through tough rhetoric even as he negotiated with the Soviet leader. He also used the speech to impress on Gorbachev Washington's insistence that the Soviets take responsibility for promoting positive change in Eastern Europe.

The tough words were soon forgotten in a rush of improved relations. In December 1987 Gorbachev visited Washington. As he walked the streets, crowds of well-wishers rushed to shake his hand. At a White House ceremony, he and Reagan signed a landmark treaty completely eliminating intermediate-range missiles from their arsenals. Despite the good feelings, Reagan shocked Gorbachev as well as some of his own advisers by telling off-color anti-Soviet jokes during a meeting with the Russian. Secretary of State Shultz, who pulled the president aside for a scolding, decided that Reagan's mental agility had slipped and that he should not be allowed to meet foreign leaders without supervision.

In May 1988 Reagan finally visited the Soviet Union. Speaking to a crowd in Red Square, Reagan answered a question about how he felt visiting the "evil empire." "I was talking about another time, another era," he responded.[35] Meanwhile, both Gorbachev and Colin Powell wondered how the two nations would adjust to "losing" their "best enemy."

During 1988 Gorbachev repeatedly urged Reagan to join him in making deeper cuts in nuclear arsenals, establishing a transition government in Afghanistan, and opening peace talks in Central America and Africa. Most Americans strongly supported this conciliatory approach, but Reagan appeared stung by verbal attacks from some unrepentant anticommunist conservatives who condemned him as a "useful idiot" in the Soviet conspiracy because of his cooperation with Gorbachev. Whether out of political caution or fatigue, he spurned Gorbachev's appeals and ran out the clock on domestic and foreign policy. This reluctance to cooperate had especially dire consequences in Afghanistan following the withdrawal of Soviet troops.

Flush with success in reducing Cold War hostility, Reagan left office one of the most popular presidents in post–World War II America, with an approval rating of about 70 percent. Democrats and Republicans alike credited him with turning the page on decades of confrontation. Polling data showed that Americans held Mikhail Gorbachev in even higher regard. *Time* magazine, an arbiter of American opinion, selected Gorbachev as its "Man of the Year" in 1988. Two years later, *Time* again passed over Reagan to honor Gorbachev as "man of the decade."

5

Legacies

Shortly before he left office in January 1989, Reagan described what he considered his political legacy. When the "Left" took over the Democratic Party, he explained, "we" conservatives took over the Republican Party. "We made [the GOP] into the party of the working people, the family, the neighborhood, the defense of freedom, and yes, the American flag and the Pledge of Allegiance to one nation under God." Reagan insisted that Republicans now embodied the old virtues of the Democratic Party and he asked that "all Americans come home and join me." But this vision of a permanent Republican majority fell well short of the mark.

Although Reagan won election twice, and by an especially wide margin in 1984, his average popularity over eight years was just about the same as the two other post-1945 two-term presidents, Dwight D. Eisenhower and Bill Clinton. Reagan's approval numbers spiked just before the 1984 election and again as he left office in 1989. On average his approval rating stood at 54 percent, compared to Clinton's average of 55 percent.

Since 1989 Reagan's reputation has seesawed, and his legacy remains contested. The waning of the Cold War after 1989 and the peaceful liberation of Eastern Europe, followed by the surprisingly nonviolent dissolution of the Soviet Union in 1991, provided Reagan with a large measure of good will. He, rather than his successor, George H. W. Bush, gleaned much of the credit for this historic change.

Reagan certainly shifted American political discourse to the right. His description of government as "a problem" in the lives of ordinary Americans and his condemnation of taxes and regulations had an impact on both major parties and on government at all levels. Some have called antitax rhetoric "Reagan's revenge," since the loss of revenue and chronic deficits (except for the Clinton years) tied the hands of his successors who might want to initiate new federal programs.

Reagan's legislative achievements, outside of the early tax cuts and defense spending increases, were quite modest. Social and religious conservatives celebrated him as a foe of abortion, an advocate of school prayer, and a champion of what they called "traditional family values," but he never expended much effort in getting Congress to address these issues through either legislation or constitutional amendment. Privately, leaders of the Christian Right seethed at his failure to push their agenda.

In spite of promises to shrink federal spending, the size of government, and the deficit, all grew larger under Reagan. Federal income tax rates were cut modestly for most Americans, but payroll and state taxes increased by about the same amount. When he left office, taxes accounted for nearly the same proportion of the national economy (a bit over 19 percent) as when he entered. What had happened, however, was a substantial reduction in the tax liability of the richest 20 percent of Americans and the advent of chronic annual budget deficits in the range of $200 billion.

Reagan's much-ballyhooed "war on drugs" substantially boosted the state and federal prison populations but had little impact on patterns or rates of drug use. He all but ignored the growing AIDS epidemic while promoting abstinence-only sex education for school children. Meanwhile, despite his repeated emphasis on traditional family values, the rates of divorce and out-of-wedlock births increased.

Reagan succeeded in broadening the base of the Republican Party. He cemented alliances between economic and social conservatives as well as between large numbers of Protestant Evangelicals and conservative Catholics, who had traditionally mistrusted each other. Richard Nixon had built up a strong GOP following among formerly Democratic white Southerners, but Reagan solidified the so-called Southern Strategy. In fact, by the time he left office, the formerly Democratic South became the most Republican region of the country. These developments assured the Republicans a near majority of support in many state and federal elections since the early 1990s. Over time, this also made the GOP a much more conservative party than it had been when Reagan was first elected. In the 1990s and beyond, many Republicans rejected Reagan's willingness to compromise with Democrats to enact desired legislation.

Reagan's appointment of over 400 federal judges, all of whom enjoyed lifetime tenure, had a dramatic and ongoing impact on the courts and broader justice system. His four Supreme Court appointments (William Rehnquist, promoted to Chief Justice, and Associate Justices Sandra Day O'Connor, Antonin Scalia, and Anthony Kennedy) moved the judiciary in a more conservative direction on issues such as criminal law; privacy rights; race, age, and gender discrimination; and the role of religion in public life.

After Reagan returned to California in 1989, the glow that surrounded his success in ratcheting down the Cold War began to fade. The collapse of the savings and loan industry in the early 1990s, due in large part to deregulation and tax changes pushed by Reagan, cost the Treasury about $200 billion in bailouts. Reagan's successor, President George H. W. Bush, bore the brunt of criticism for the problem, but Reagan had his own share of censure for his role in the collapse. Bush also presided over growing budget deficits, caused largely by Reagan's and his own anti-tax pledges.

Reagan made few public appearances during the Bush years. He said little about the political upheavals in Eastern Europe, the Soviet Union, and China between 1989 and 1992. Perhaps embarrassed by his support for Saddam Hussein in the 1980s, Reagan ducked questions about the lead-up to the 1991 United States–led Gulf War against Iraq. The ex-president did occasionally make paid speeches to foreign business groups, such as a Japanese corporation that paid him a multimillion-dollar fee for a few minutes of his time. Since ex-presidents receive generous pensions and other benefits, this struck many Americans as unseemly.

The economic recession of 1991–92 and Bush's abandonment of his "no new taxes" pledge led many Americans to ponder if the Reagan era was really over. When Democrat

Bill Clinton captured the White House in 1992, Reagan's dream of a "permanent Republican majority" seemed deferred, if not ended. To bolster Reagan's legacy, congressional Republicans endorsed the "Reagan Legacy Project," which resulted in naming Washington's airport, the largest federal building in the capital, an aircraft carrier, and many local schools after the ex-president. There have also been many proposals to memorialize Reagan by putting his face on paper currency, perhaps by displacing President and Civil War hero Ulysses S. Grant from the $50 bill. The election of George W. Bush in 2000 and 2004, as well as continued GOP control of Congress until 2006, affirmed the underlying strength of the post-Reagan Republican Party.

In November 1994 Reagan revealed to the public, in a moving letter he composed himself, that he had been diagnosed with Alzheimer's disease and would soon pass into the "sunset of my life." But for America, he added, there would always be a "bright dawn ahead." During the next decade, sheltered by his wife, Reagan withdrew from sight and descended into a fog of dementia. Some historians and especially journalists who covered Reagan during his presidency have speculated whether his occasional lapses of lucidity, some dating from his first administration, might have been early symptoms of Alzheimer's. However, doctors who examined him during his presidency reported no evidence of impairment.

Reagan indirectly affected the outcome of the 2000 presidential election. The justices he had named to the Supreme Court—Rehnquist (promoted to Chief Justice), Kennedy, O'Connor, and Scalia—provided four of the five votes that secured the contested Florida election, and thus the White House, for George W. Bush. The younger Bush proved a more faithful heir to Reagan than had his more politically moderate father. "W" resurrected several Reagan-era initiatives, including tax cuts tilted heavily in favor of the rich, aggressive deregulation of financial institutions, and deployment of an antimissile system. Bush also partly justified his militant response to the terrorist attacks of September 11, 2001 as "Reaganesque."

Reagan's death on June 5, 2004 elicited an outpouring of national emotion, as politicians from both parties claimed parts of his mantle. Many Americans fondly recalled Reagan's ability to sell a policy with a smile rather than with invective. Barack Obama recognized the continued appeal of this quality. As a Democratic presidential candidate in 2008, he praised Reagan's skill at "tapping into what people were already feeling" and presenting to them a clear set of ideas about government. Above all, Obama asserted, Reagan offered Americans "optimism" and a "return to that sense of dynamism and entrepreneurship that had been missing" since the "excesses of the '60s and '70s."

Because his presidency remains such a polarizing subject, Ronald Reagan is, and will continue to be, a fascinating political leader, a visionary hero to some and a cartoonish buffoon or villain to others. No matter how drastically opinions differ, few could contest Reagan's profound and lasting influence on American politics, certainly still in evidence today. When he entered politics as a candidate for governor of California in 1966, he quipped that he saw his new profession as a form of show business: "You have a hell of an opening, coast for a while, and then have a hell of a close."[36] In ways he probably never imagined, Reagan's public life followed this trajectory.

Notes

1. Garry Wills, "Mr. Magoo Remembers," *New York Review of Books*, Dec. 20, 1990, 29.

2. Garry Wills, *Reagan's America* (1987), 445.

3. Peggy Noonan, *What I Saw at the Revolution: A Political Life in the Reagan Era* (1990), 154.

4. Haynes Johnson, *Sleepwalking through History: America in the Reagan Years* (1992), 60.

5. Lou Cannon, *President Reagan: The Role of a Lifetime* (1991; repr. 2000), 487–491.

6. Reagan's role in the 1940 film *Murder in the Air* and its similarity to aspects of the Strategic Defense Initiative of 1983 are discussed extensively in Wills, *Reagan's*

America, Frances Fitzgerald, *Way Out There in the Blue: Reagan, Star Wars, and the End of the Cold War* (2000), and Michael Rogin, *Ronald Reagan: The Movie and Other Episodes in Political Demonology* (1987).

7. Michael Reagan, *On the Outside Looking In* (1988); Maureen Reagan, *First Father, First Daughter* (1989); Patti Davis Reagan, *Homefront* (1986) and *The Way I See It* (1992).

8. The best single study of "Sunbelt conservatism," especially in California, is by Lisa McGirr, *Suburban Warriors: The Origins of the New American Right* (2002).

9. On the rise of Barry Goldwater and Reagan's involvement on his behalf, see Rick Perlstein, *Before the Storm: Barry Goldwater and the Unmaking of the American Consensus* (2001).

10. William E. Pemberton, *Exit with Honor: The Life and Presidency of Ronald Reagan* (1997; repr. 1998), 69.

11. The best study of Reagan's election as governor of California and its impact on national politics is Matthew Dallek, *The Right Moment: Ronald Reagan's First Victory and the Decisive Turning Point in American Politics* (2000).

12. Lou Cannon, *Governor Reagan: His Rise to Power* (2003), 172–173.

13. Pemberton, *Exit With Honor,* 70.

14. For Reagan's style of governing and his legislative accomplishments, see Cannon, *Governor Reagan.*

15. Drafts and completed versions of many of Reagan's commentaries are reprinted in Kiron Skinner, Annelise Anderson, and Martin Anderson, eds., *Reagan in His Own Hand: The Writings of Ronald Reagan That Reveal His Revolutionary Vision for America* (2001).

16. The impact on domestic politics of the debate over the Panama Canal Treaty is discussed by Adam Clymer in *Drawing the Line at the Big Ditch: The Panama Canal Treaties and the Rise of the Right* (2008).

17. Pemberton, *Exit with Honor*, 89.

18. For a discussion of how the White House staff managed Reagan's image, see Michael K. Deaver, with Mickey Hershkowitz, *Behind the Scenes* (1987). The supine role of the press is examined in Mark Hertsgaard, *On Bended Knee: The Press and the Reagan Presidency* (1988).

19. For a discussion of Reagan's decision-making style, see Martin Anderson, *Revolution: The Reagan Legacy* (1990), 289–291.

20. For a description of how the White House staff produced many of Reagan's memorable quotes, see Larry Speakes, *Speaking Out: The Reagan Presidency from Inside the White House* (1988).

21. In 1983, faced with a deficit in the Social Security trust fund that paid pensions to retired workers, Reagan appointed a bipartisan commission. Its solution, accepted by Congress and the president, involved gradually raising

the retirement age, reducing some benefits, and increasing payroll taxes that funded the program. This plugged the shortfall but increased the tax burden on most working- and middle-class Americans.

22. Watt proved such an extremist that his policies provoked an environmental backlash that boosted membership in groups like the Sierra Club. Reagan fired the interior secretary in late 1983, following a series of racial gaffes and his refusal to let the Beach Boys perform at a concert on the National Mall. Watt had not known that the 1960s surfer band was a personal favorite of Nancy Reagan.

23. When Congress ultimately enacted a King holiday in 1983, Reagan signed the law with great fanfare and praised King's contribution to American justice.

24. Reagan, a nonsmoker, had appeared in many cigarette ads during the 1940s and 1950s.

25. Pemberton, *Exit With Honor,* 154.

26. *The New York Times,* July 17, 1980.

27. Despite his anger at Nixon's opening of Communist China in 1971, Reagan, as president, muted his criticism of Beijing and cooperated with China in providing aid to anti-Soviet guerrillas in Afghanistan. He justified this as a tactic to confront the main communist threat coming from Moscow.

28. The most compelling evidence that the Reagan "hard line" did little to change Soviet policy is provided by Beth A. Fischer, *The Reagan Reversal: Foreign Policy and the End of the Cold War* (2000); Raymond Garthoff, *Great Transition: American–Soviet Relations and the End of the Cold War* (1994); and Don Oberdorfer, *From the Cold War to a New Era: The United States and the Soviet Union, 1983–1991* (1998).

29. For an exhaustive study of the origins and impact of SDI, see Frances Fitzgerald, *Way Out There in the Blue: Reagan, Star Wars, and the End of the Cold War* (2000).

30. As Soviet and many American critics concluded, the laser-powered missile shield in space proved impossible to build. Two decades later, under President George W. Bush, the United States began deployment of a limited, ground-based antimissile system unrelated to the Reagan-era program and directed against "rogue" states such as North Korea and Iran.

31. Robert C. McFarlane (with Zofia Smardz), *Special Trust* (1994), 68. Two of the best studies of Iran-Contra are Jane Mayer and Doyle McManus, *Landslide: The Unmaking of the President, 1984–1988* (1988), and Theodore Draper, *A Very Thin Line: The Iran-Contra Affair* (1991).

32. A discussion of the interplay between Reagan and those most involved in Iran-Contra can be found in

the retrospective account of the special prosecutor. See Joseph E. Walsh, *Firewall: The Iran-Contra Conspiracy and Cover-Up* (1997).

33. Reagan had exchanged formal messages and a few personal letters with Soviet leaders from 1981 to 1985, but nothing came of them.

34. On efforts by Nancy Reagan, Suzanne Massey, and Joan Quigley to convince Reagan to meet with Gorbachev, see Nancy Reagan, *My Turn: The Memoirs of Nancy Reagan* (1989); Joan Quigley, *"What Does Joan Say?" My Seven Years as White House Astrologer to Nancy and Ronald Reagan* (1990); and James Mann, *The Rebellion of Ronald Reagan: A History of the End of the Cold War* (2009). Mann stresses that Reagan's anxieties about nuclear weapons pushed him toward cooperation with Gorbachev.

35. Oberdorfer, *From the Cold War to a New Era,* 299.

36. Sean Wilentz, *The Age of Reagan: A History* (2008), 127.

Bibliography

Primary Sources

Reagan's presidential papers are deposited at the Ronald Reagan Presidential Library, a branch of the National Archives and Record Service's presidential library system, located in Simi Valley, California. Reagan's pre- and post-presidential ghostwritten memoirs—Reagan with Richard Gipson Hubler, *Where's the Rest of Me?* (1965; repr. 1981), and Reagan, *An American Life* (1990; repr. 1992)—are not especially reliable or informative. Somewhat more revealing is Reagan's presidential diary, although it provides more a record of events than a self-reflective view of his official actions. See Douglas Brinkley, ed., *The Reagan Diaries Unabridged: Vol. 1: January 1981–October 1985; Vol. 2: November 1985–January 1989* (2009). Much of the diary is also accessible online through the Reagan Library website listed below. Two edited collections of Reagan's personal letters and radio commentaries reveal a good deal about his political values, friendships, and evolution as a public figure. See Kiron Skinner, Annelise Anderson, and Martin Anderson, eds., *Reagan in His Own Hand: The Writings of Ronald Reagan That Reveal His Revolutionary Vision for America* (2001), and Kiron Skinner, Annelise Anderson, and Martin Anderson, eds., *Reagan: A Life in Letters* (2003).

Memoirs by family members include: Nancy Reagan, *My Turn: The Memoirs of Nancy Reagan* (1989); Michael Reagan, *On the Outside Looking In* (1988); Maureen Reagan, *First Father, First Daughter* (1989); Patti Davis Reagan, *Homefront* (1986) and *The Way I See It* (1992). See also Joan Quigley, *"What Does Joan Say?" My Seven Years as White House Astrologer to Nancy and Ronald Reagan* (1990).

Among the memoirs written by Reagan's aides or others who served in his administration, the most useful include: Martin Anderson, *Revolution: The Reagan Legacy* (1990); Terrell Bell, *The Thirteenth Man: A Reagan Cabinet Memoir* (1988); Michael K. Deaver, with Mickey

Hershkowitz, *Behind the Scenes* (1987); Alexander Haig, *Caveat: Realism, Reagan, and Foreign Policy* (1984); Jack F. Matlock, *Reagan and Gorbachev: How the Cold War Ended* (2004); Robert C. McFarlane (with Zofia Smardz), *Special Trust* (1994); Edwin Meese, *With Reagan: The Inside Story* (1992); Peggy Noonan, *What I Saw at the Revolution: A Political Life in the Reagan Era* (1990); Oliver North with William Novak, *Under Fire: An American Story* (1991); Colin Powell with Joseph E. Persico, *My American Journey* (1995); Donald T. Reagan, *For the Record: From Wall Street to Washington* (1988); George Shultz, *Turmoil and Triumph: Diplomacy, Power and the Triumph of the American Ideal* (1993); Larry Speakes, *Speaking Out: The Reagan Presidency from Inside the White House* (1988); David A. Stockman, *The Triumph of Politics: How the Reagan Revolution Failed* (1986); Joseph E. Walsh, *Firewall: The Iran-Contra Conspiracy and Cover-Up* (1997); James Watt, *The Courage of a Conservative* (1985); and Casper Weinberger, *Fighting for Peace: Seven Critical Years in the Pentagon* (1990).

Secondary Sources

Reagan's authorized biography by Edmund Morris, *Dutch: A Memoir of Ronald Reagan* (1999), disappointed nearly everyone with its odd mix of fictional and factual characters and dubious speculation about Reagan's life. Fortunately, there are several excellent biographies that cover Reagan's early life and political career. Among the best are: Lou Cannon, *President Reagan: The Role of a Lifetime* (1991; repr. 2000), *Governor Reagan: His Rise to Power* (2003), and *Ronald Reagan: A Life in Politics* (2004); Robert Dallek, *Ronald Reagan: The Politics of Symbolism* (1984); Haynes Bonner Johnson, *Sleepwalking Through History: America in the Reagan Years* (1992); Chester Pach, *The Presidency of Ronald Reagan* (2011); William E. Pemberton, *Exit with Honor: The Life and Presidency of Ronald Reagan* (1997; repr. 1998); Michael Schaller, *Reckoning with Reagan: America and Its President in the 1980s* (1992); Sean Wilentz, *The Age of Reagan: A History* (2008); and Garry Wills, *Reagan's America: Innocents at Home* (1987; repr. 2000).

Insightful studies of the forces that shaped Reagan's ideas and policies both before and during his presidency include: Andrew Busch, *Reagan's Victory: The Presidential Election of 1980 and the Rise of the Right* (2005); Steve Coll, *Ghost Wars: The Secret History of the CIA, Afghanistan, and Bin Laden from the Soviet Invasion to September 10, 2001* (2004); Adam Clymer, *Drawing the Line at the Big Ditch: The Panama Canal Treaties and the Rise of the Right* (2008); Matthew Dallek, *The Right Moment: Ronald Reagan's First Victory and the Decisive Turning Point in American Politics* (2000); Theodore Draper, *A Very Thin*

Line: *The Iran-Contra Affair* (1991); Steve Emmerson, *Secret Warriors: Inside the Covert Military Operations of the Reagan Administration* (1988); John Ehrman, *The Eighties: America in the Age of Reagan* (2005); Beth A. Fischer, *The Reagan Reversal: Foreign Policy and the End of the Cold War* (2000); Frances Fitzgerald, *Way Out There in the Blue: Reagan, Star Wars, and the End of the Cold War* (2000); Raymond Garthoff, *Great Transition: American–Soviet Relations and the End of the Cold War* (1994); Seven Hayward, *The Age of Reagan: The Conservative Counter-revolution, 1980–1989;* Steven Hayward, *The Age of Reagan: The Fall of the Old Liberal Order, 1964–1980;* Mark Hertsgaard, *On Bended Knee: The Press and the Reagan Presidency* (1988); Kyle Longley, ed., *Deconstructing Reagan: Conservative Mythology and America's Fortieth President* (2006); Lisa McGirr, *Suburban Warriors: The Origins of the New American Right* (2002); James Mann, *The Rebellion of Ronald Reagan: A History of the End of the Cold War* (2009); Jane Mayer and Doyle McManus, *Landslide: The Unmaking of the President, 1984–1988* (1988); Martin Mayer, *The Greatest Bank Job Ever: The Collapse of the Savings and Loan Industry* (1990); John Micklethwait and Adrian Wooldridge, *The Right Nation: Conservative Power in America* (2004); Don Oberdorfer, *From the Cold War to a New Era: The United States and the Soviet Union, 1983–1991* (1998); Rick Perlstein, *Before the Storm: Barry Goldwater and the Unmaking of the American Consensus* (2001); Kevin Phillips, *The Politics of Rich and Poor: Wealth and the American Electorate in the Reagan Aftermath* (1990); Michael Rogin, *Ronald Reagan: The Movie and Other Episodes in Political Demonology* (1987); Herman Schwartz, *Packing the Courts: The Conservative Drive to Rewrite the Constitution* (1988); Bruce Shulman, *The Seventies: The Great Shift in American Culture, Society and Politics* (2001); John W. Sloan, *The Reagan Effect: Economics and Presidential Leadership* (1999); and Gil Troy, *Morning in America: How Ronald Reagan Invented the 1980s* (2007).

Online Resources

The website of The Ronald Reagan Presidential Library, http://www.reaganlibrary.net, provides links to many of Reagan's important speeches, his diary, and other interesting textual and visual material.

Other Books by Michael Schaller

Right Turn: American Life in the Reagan-Bush Era, 1980–1992

Reckoning with Reagan: America and Its President in the 1980s

The Republican Ascendancy: American Politics, 1968–2001
(with George Rising)

Present Tense: The United States Since 1945
(with Karen Anderson and Robert D. Schulzinger)

Coming of Age: America in the Twentieth Century
(with Virginia Scharff and Robert D. Schulzinger)